The Journey to Sales Transformation

25 AXIOMS FOR BECOMING
A TRUSTED PARTNER TO YOUR CUSTOMERS

BOB NICOLS JR.

with Bob Sanders and Michael S. Mann

ABSTRACT

A chief sales officer finds that sales transformation can be achieved by learning ways to answer "yes" to twenty-five simple questions. His journey is directed by a crafty old messenger who reveals the truth about becoming a "trusted partner" to his customers through observations and stories about a tartar sauce-making county commission chairman, a 1965 Ford Mustang, a British talent show judge, an African wise man, a homebuilder, two Little League baseball coaches, and Sir Isaac Newton.

ISBN: 1466388552
ISBN-13: 9781466388550
Library of Congress Control Number: 2011917996

CreateSpace, North Charleston, SC

Dedicated to my parents

Robert W. Nicols Sr., for your gifts of unconditional love, patience, wisdom, faith, and the sense of undeniable logic that creates the foundation for everything in this book. I can still hear you telling me as a young boy "You can do anything you choose to do". This book is proof that I believe you.

And

Ethel Marie Nicols for your gifts of unconditional love, sense of humor and appreciation of music. Thank you for not only being my mother, but a best friend. You have been my biggest cheerleader since the day I was born.

Your 66 years of marriage (and counting) are a shining example.

I love you both with all my heart.

And

My Children, Geoffrey Robert Nicols and Hannah Marie Nicols, for the sacrifices you made as your dad traveled and built a business. I love you unconditionally and forever.

Table of Contents

CHAPTER 1

A Chief Sales Officer Bites the Dust

Looking out the window didn't help. David Malone took it all in from his corner office on the tenth floor. The almost-cloudless, bright blue sky, the constant flow of activity on the street below, and the tree-filled park just two blocks away would usually brighten his spirits. This particular Friday morning it just postponed the inevitable.

The mounting problems he faced weren't to be found outside his window. They were right there inside his office, and that's where the solutions would have to be, too. So he sighed, smiled a good-bye to anything beautiful for a while, and turned around to face the realities and responsibilities of the job that provided him with that normally inspiring view.

Being the chief sales officer of a stalled technology company didn't allow for anything except solving problems—or at least attempting to solve problems—with shareholders and a board of directors who were growing, as was David, more impatient with the company's lackluster performance. It had been several months of frenzied pace and missed scenic city vistas as he tried everything he thought might get the company's sales numbers jump-started, but nothing helped—and nothing hurt, either.

1

I wonder, he thought, *if there'd be a bit of difference if I'd come to work and just sat here looking out the window all day long every day.* Whatever he tried, from something as simple as an encouraging pat on the back for a hard-working salesperson to something as complex as formulating global sales strategies, the result was never more than a barely noticeable twitch in the monthly report.

It also seemed like there wasn't any relief coming around any corner. Customers continued to demand ever-higher service level agreements and ever-lower pricing. The word "commodity" increasingly crept into conversations between salespeople and customers. David knew that keeping up with competitors meant discovering a new approach, new ways to apply technology, new ways to package their services, and new ways to manage, motivate, and compensate his sales staff.

The checklist of what he thought would provide solutions replayed in his mind as an endless loop, actions he was certain at the time would right the course so wind would fill the sails of the stalled ship he captained. As tight as budgets had been, any one of those initiatives would have been considered a significant accomplishment by most. Under his leadership, the company implemented sophisticated activity reporting with salesforce automation. Human resources started using new hiring profiles to help identify ideal sales and management candidates. A new sales compensation program with accelerators and margin incentives was launched with great fanfare and greater anticipation. Online sales and product training was developed and delivered to field staff on brand-new laptops. None of it mattered.

He had pushed hard for the board of directors to invest in product development, and the company had focused a ton of human and financial resources trying to develop the newest version of the latest and greatest. New products and services were being released almost every month, but by the time of the release the company was already working on the "Next Next Big Thing" to replace it and keep pace with the competition. In the technology era, "new" seemed to stay new about as long as a loaf of bakery bread stayed fresh after the twist tie disappeared.

While David felt he had done a great deal for the people in the trenches, field morale was terrible. The salespeople had clamored for more and better and faster, but the pace of new releases was way too fast for the company's HR department to get people in the field adequately trained on each new improvement. Systems and support lagged woefully behind the pace of invention. And while sales force automation was sorely needed, most salespeople felt every keystroke of data entry represented lost time in front of customers.

Salespeople were still selling only the products they knew, while management was trying to force-feed the company's new industry-leading technology and programs—the Next Big Thing du jour—by conducting sales blitzes and special promotions.

Then there were the company's customers.

David mumbled to himself, *"Every prospect, every customer is in survival mode."* They had all developed tunnel vision, protecting, nurturing, and growing their own businesses. No one had the time or inclination to go on an expensive fishing expedition, hoping to hook some new technology that might have the *potential* to benefit their business. Customers had seen enough Next Big Things and were tired of being told they needed the newest technology. They had developed an attitude toward salespeople that said, *"Don't come to me when YOU think your technology is ready. Come to me when you know I'm ready for your technology."*

The pace was relentless, and though the efforts produced some momentarily significant advances, the company's expenses skyrocketed while sales remained grounded as if spectators to the continuous change.

A fresh copy of his résumé shone on the monitor of his home computer, a glowing reminder of his failures.

David didn't have to be in a hurry any more. In fact, his afternoon would be spent waiting, or doing the little things people do to occupy themselves when waiting is the most important thing on their agenda. He took a quick glance over his shoulder at the desk that sometimes felt as if it was an extra appendage he'd need a team of surgeons to remove. Today, he knew there were seven surgeons assembled on the far corner of the tenth floor with a window offering them the same gorgeous view he was enjoying.

The board of directors was, he knew, at that very moment discussing amputating his appendage, permanently. By the end of business, he would most likely be David Alan Malone, *former* chief sales officer. Yes, many of the investments the company made at David's urging were needed. Some might even be considered noble. But the effort had been a gamble, and he'd lost.

The directors, like David, knew the company's struggles couldn't be blamed solely on the pace of advances in technology or a questionable economy. His sales organization simply wasn't producing, and the board discussed the need to revamp and retool the sales effort to find a means of increasing both sales revenue and profit margins. There had to be a sales transformation.

David had his opportunity and didn't get the job done. It wasn't hard for the Board to figure out. They had warned and counseled David about the consequences of a weak sales performance on numerous occasions. While they approved the budget for each of his programs, David and his organization were responsible for the execution with successful results. It just didn't happen. Change was in order, and of the magnitude that would require new leadership, new direction.

The door to David Malone's office opened quietly and was just as quiet when Hannah Marie Bergman, CEO and chairman of the board, stepped in and closed it behind her. It had been a little over four hours since the Board began its meeting, and from the look on Chairman Bergman's face, it couldn't have been an easy four hours. David spun his chair away from the window and back toward his usual position facing the desk, at least for a few minutes more.

The chairman dropped into a chair across the desk, her eyes never leaving David's. "You know, David, we had hoped you would be able to turn this thing around by now. We talked about what got us into this position, and we're certainly not going to place the blame entirely on you," Bergman said.

"Feels like that's about to happen," David said, with a smile to let the chairman know everything was really okay.

"Yeah, that's the way things work," Bergman said, returning David's smile with one considerably less comfortable. "The board decided not to wait any longer. We need to get the company moving in the right direction quickly, and lately it hasn't been moving in any direction at all. It's time for a change, a true transformation.

"We've decided we need a new chief sales officer."

"Well, Hannah, it's too bad I can't show you reports that would let me argue with you, but we're all looking at the same numbers. Wish I could have done a better job for you."

"David, nobody's ever questioned your desire, and every single member of the board mentioned how hard you work and how easy you are to work with. I want to let you know that the board's vote wasn't unanimous, and it wasn't easy for anybody in the room. Nobody wanted to do it, but the consensus of the board is that it's necessary to do something now."

"I understand," he said. "And, if you would, Hannah, tell the others I really appreciate the opportunity I was given and there are no hard feelings at all from me. I hope you find somebody that can provide the spark I haven't been able to."

"Thank you, David. I'll be sure to tell them."

The chairman explained the severance package the board had agreed to offer, which was more than satisfactory to David. They decided the now-former CSO would be at the chairman and CEO's office at eleven the next morning to sign paperwork, hand over keys, and complete all the other steps to close that chapter of David's life.

And with that, they each rose, shook hands, and walked toward the door. Normally they would have said goodbye, and David would have returned to his desk. Today's surgery offered him freedom from that physically and emotionally exhausting appendage. They walked out together, the chairman turning left toward the board-room and David turning right toward the elevators to take him down the eleven flights to the building's underground garage. He'd hop in his car and take a leisurely drive home, maybe even stop at the park and watch some kids play. It had been so long since he hadn't been in a hurry and he thought watching kids play ball was a perfect way to celebrate.

With that decision finalized, business continued on as business usually does. While the seat of former CSO David Malone's office chair was still warm, the board conversation turned to discussions of his replacement. The company needed a new and more effec-tive chief sales officer immediately because a company and sales organization can't survive long without leadership and direction. The board definitely wanted to be certain it would make the right selection, but all seven members knew it had to be as quick as pos-sible, within reason.

First, Chairman Bergman set the extremes of a broad spectrum of possibilities where they might find the person who could right the company's wayward sales course. She asked if anyone knew of a potential rising star or whether there was a veteran out there with a long history of making sales departments perform as expected.

"Any ideas, anyone?"

It was very similar to the way the board of directors had approached the search when it had chosen David just three years before. The search was officially on.

CHAPTER 2

Two CSO Candidates Collide

Phillip Evan Hawthorne was the rising star. He was a predator, and he was hungry.

He had been circling high overhead, just watching and waiting for the right moment to begin to launch into a dive. He didn't wait for his prey to die, but just until it couldn't fight any longer. With his head pointed toward the earth and his wings tucked tight in aerodynamic perfection, Phillip rarely missed his target.

The company was sick and weak, anyone could tell that by looking at published performance figures, but the numbers didn't explain *why* the company was unhealthy. The product portfolio was compelling and, if anything, could actually be pared back for stronger focus and greater efficiency. But the leading-edge products were strong, their pricing was competitive, and the company's reputation for service was at least adequate. During interviews for the CSO position, Phillip would have to make a point of letting the company know the first priority would be to provide strong sales and marketing leadership. The second would be to establish new recruiting, hiring, and training procedures as he began to churn the bottom half of an apparently ineffective sales staff.

Improvement from the top down and bottom up would speed up the process of the company's sales revival.

Phillip Evan Hawthorne's star had been rising at the tech giant where he worked before, but it was limited there. It wouldn't reach its apex soon enough for Phillip, and maybe never, if he stayed. The aggressive, independent hunter mentality that had started developing at the age of twelve when he lost his father in a car accident, had always served him well professionally and personally. Unfortunately, it had the side effect of creating some enemies along the way, especially among the kind of people who seemed like they could forgive anything but someone else's success. And perhaps his biggest liability was a birth certificate in a company that valued experience over youthful production. Phillip felt he had demonstrated, on a daily basis, that he had all the skills needed to be that company's CSO, but the youngest chief-level executive in company history, the person the board of directors considered young blood, was at forty-eight more than a decade older than Phillip.

His relative youth and history of internal company politics might have dimmed his chances of reaching the coveted CSO status at his current place of employment, but from outside the company looking in, his work appeared without a single blemish. It hadn't been uncommon for other companies to inquire about his interest in joining them, and he'd even given a couple of them more than a cursory glance before politely rebuffing their interest. Then this company in dire need of his energy and skill had aggressively sought him out and made him one of the two final candidates to become chief sales officer. It wasn't the giant his current company had become, but this new one certainly had the potential to grow.

And from the perspective of a salesman who carried the genes of two parents who were themselves very successful salespeople, Phillip knew that what this company needed more than anything was new, young, aggressive, forward-thinking leadership. As a matter fact, he thought it could have been a slogan printed in embossed lettering on his business cards. Since the last year of his master's program, Phillip's goal had been to reach the C-level of management by his fortieth birthday. Getting this job would beat that timetable by a little over two years and simultaneously let his current employer see what a terrible mistake in judgment it had made by not providing their rising star with an opportunity befitting his enormous potential that no one, especially Phillip himself, doubted would be filled in an ever-rising career arc.

There was just one more step, one final stage of this new company's interview process. The job was his. He felt it inside, as if destiny had provided him with a map of his life that showed this was his road to success. He knew in his core being that Phillip Evan Hawthorne was exactly what this company needed to lead its sales revenues to new heights. And he knew the Board interviewing him would easily recognize that as well as it compared him to the only other candidate for the CSO position who would have to come out of retirement to take the job.

The one person temporarily delaying Phillip from achieving his destiny couldn't have been a worse selection considering the company's needs, at least the way Phillip saw it.

The old guy is so far past his prime, he might not even remember it. Not only is it unlikely that he's "transformed" anything, he doesn't have experience in the technology sector. Add to that the fact that he had an extremely conservative background when the company needed an innovator like, well, Phillip. Certainly every single difference in the two finalists screamed out that he was the right man for the right job at the right time.

Phillip was honest enough with himself to recognize his competition for the position didn't show up at the table empty-handed. His company's sales performances had always been consistent. Ho-hum. And while sales had grown steadily, no single year had shown anything dramatic. And why would it? He'd supposedly had the same salespeople forever. Phillip couldn't deny his experience,

9

though. He'd been a successful sales leader at his company since before Yoko told John to imagine there's no Beatles. The guy had a reputation as a great storyteller, but the only stories he could possibly tell more likely included references to the first spaceships being launched rather than sales campaigns for leading-edge technology.

This company needed new blood and the energy, vitality, and a few good, swift Hawthorne kicks to the right rear ends for a quick turnaround. As the new chief sales officer, Phillip knew he'd be leading the way at a pace almost intimidating to the people working under him. This would likely be at the time every afternoon when his elderly competition for the job would be asking his secretary to keep the noise down for her boss's afternoon nap. Ask Phillip on the day of his interview and he'd have offered his opinion that the other candidate was the kind of executive who guaranteed the company's ready-to-explode technology would never have a matching sales explosion; the kind of person who would doom the company to remain in its present, undesirable financial position that had caused the search for a new chief sales officer in the first place.

"Would you come out of retirement?"

He suddenly felt like an NFL coach with his hand gripping the red flag in his pocket—Ben's brain immediately felt the urge to call for a review of the play. He ran the replays from every angle at regular speed, slow motion, and then frozen for closer examination before finally deciding the ruling on the field was confirmed. Thankfully the process couldn't have taken two full seconds, unlike the distractingly long time it took real NFL officials to figure out if someone's foot had been on one side of a line or the other.

Benjamin Delaney had, in fact, just been asked if he wanted to leave his life that was free of outside stress and replace it with the kinds of pressures he knew he would face leading someone's struggling sales efforts again.

He started laughing, not because the idea itself was funny, but because the timing of the question was freakishly entertaining in one of those "had-to-be-there-yourself" kind of ways. Just two days before being asked, the planned contentment of Ben's retirement had suffered its first crack.

"Maybe if the right opportunity came along, just maybe..."

So the phone rang, a conversation started, and Ben began to think about whether this might meet the "right opportunity" qualifier in his prior, not fully developed thought about his employment status. This one was more likely to meet that standard because the call was coming from an old friend, someone who was close to a member of the board of directors for a struggling technology company in search of a new person to serve as its head of sales.

"They're lost, Ben," the retiree heard. "It's like they're on the edge, and there's a very steep ledge to fall off if they take the wrong step. They need new leadership, and I think you're exactly the kind of leader they need."

Ben's retirement wasn't the result of many years of pinching pennies in preparation for the day he could finally slap on a bumper sticker about leading the retiree's life of no watches because there was no schedule to keep. Retiring wasn't what he wanted to do—it was what Ben had had to do because, just like the rising star who would eventually become his competitor, he had experienced the sting of personal loss.

For more than forty years his wife had taken care of him. Now it was his turn to care for her. The blessings of retirement were the months, weeks, and days, and finally those last treasured hours spent with the woman he'd loved for so long he couldn't remember what it was like not to. Ben told her stories, and even in her last days, when she couldn't do anything else, his love could still roll her eyes at something outrageous or funny her husband had just said. She especially loved the tales when Ben recalled their Saturday afternoons eating hot dogs at the ballpark and watching

11

Little Leaguers from T-ballers to teens, and how he had never loved baseball until he loved her. Much of their time was spent together laughing in spite of the circumstances, until the day when she couldn't hear him anymore, even as he cried at her bedside upon that very realization.

The curses of retirement were obvious. There were lost hopes and dreams, grief, loneliness, and the boredom that came from the sometime overwhelming void left behind by his wife, best friend, and companion. When he began his musing about retiring from retirement and heading back into the workforce, it was partly because with the passing of his life's love, he felt no sense of direction or purpose in his life. The friend who called might as well have said, "You're lost, Ben, and you need some new people to lead. I think this company is exactly what you need."

He'd learn more details as the interview process played out, but the description he'd gotten about the ailing company made for an easy initial diagnosis. Flat sales with rising sales costs, the commoditization of its products and services in an ever-changing industry, and domestic and global competition, were all aggravated by an unstable and unpredictable economy that combined to put the company in peril. It needed strong, stable, experienced sales leadership.

His experience didn't come from the tech sector, but Ben heard enough to understand that the factors affecting this company weren't unusual for that time and in that segment of the business world. In fact, he knew from his years in the publishing industry that the predicament wasn't really all that unusual for anyone at any time. The tech industry had just evolved into what every other mature industry had eventually become. Just because everything was different didn't mean anything had changed. Tech was not immune from the forces that affected every other type of business. If technology companies hadn't already done all that was needed to prepare for the business to compete in this environment before it even became this environment, positive results and achieving goals weren't likely to ensue.

In doing some of his usual sales probing, Ben found out his competition for this CSO position was just a kid, which was how he now thought of anyone without a head full of gray hair. The kid offered the board of directors a stark contrast to what Ben considered his strengths. He'd found out enough about him to respect Phillip's aggressive approach and what he'd been able to accomplish, including earning his position as Ben's final competition for the chief sales officer post. But younger blood with quick fixes and swift kicks that potentially generated lots of turnover wasn't all that would be needed to yank this company out of its financial doldrums. The things needed to get this ship on the right course were experience, consistency, guidance, and reason—all of which pretty much described Ben.

Maybe the stories that had become part of his reputation and the lessons of his history had found a new home. This CSO position didn't feel like it was his destiny, but Ben knew he was supposed to play some part, that this was the path his journey through life should take. As he discussed possibilities and then went through the official interview process that followed, there was a change. Ben's sense of purpose began to return, and he felt completely alive. Besides, he'd already figured out he would make a miserable retiree anyway.

Though they both brought impressive résumés to the table, one lengthy and consistent and the other shorter and undeniably meteoric, the two finalists represented both ends of the spectrum the Board desired in candidates. Phillip and Ben each knew their charm and interview skills wouldn't be what won them this job. This would be decided on philosophy and the candidate's ability to convincingly articulate its benefits. The Board of Directors would have a clear choice based on their polar-opposite styles and approaches to the solutions they'd implement to correct the company's perceived problems. Each of the seven Directors would have their personal belief that one approach to problem-solving, not necessarily which man, would be more effective than the other.

Phillip went first when the two were invited to make a final presentation to the board and other company chief executives, as Ben sat in a nearby waiting room. No one could confuse the two CSO candidates after witnessing the two highly skilled salesmen sell themselves and their philosophies to the board.

Phillip was intriguing with his depth of industry knowledge, while Ben's stories kept their attention. Phillip was so energetic and his enthusiasm was given free rein so board members had to follow his constant motion all around the room, mostly at a pace that would have been called a march if it had been just slightly more emphatic. When it was Ben's turn, they all settled back into their chairs and listened as he spun tale after tale, as comfortable as if Aunt Bea had served iced tea and cookies while Andy was telling everyone how Otis had left the front door to the jail open the night before when he checked himself into his regular cell for being drunk. Phillip's words came at his interviewers in a sharp staccato reminiscent of the sounds of a lion tamer's whip keeping the attention of the big cats. Ben's words rolled toward them like ocean swells before gently settling on them as if to provide a cool, contented respite from the day's heat.

From the outside, neither candidate could hear exactly what was being said during the other's final presentation, but there were clues at the end. Ben heard a round of applause when the curtain dropped on Phillip's act, while what Phillip heard at the conclusion of Ben's presentation was everyone sharing a warm laugh. Even though those two individual interview conclusions represented different ends of the spectrum, they surprised no one.

Minutes after Ben's presentation ended, the door to the room where Phillip Hawthorne waited opened. Ben walked through with a big, comfortable smile and Chairman Bergman by his side.

Both candidates were informed that, even though there would be no final decision and offer that day, the board did want the two gentlemen to wait for a while in case there were questions from the seven people whose collective wisdom would help determine each of their life's paths.

As immediately as the door clicked shut behind Chairman Bergman as she returned to the boardroom discussion, the differences in the two men left waiting began to crystallize. Ben spotted a leather chair that looked like as if it had made by the same company as the chairs in the boardroom. If felt like somebody had scanned his entire body, fed the data into a computer, and designed and built the chair to fit Ben's comfort requirements perfectly.

Phillip's always-abundant energy level had been stimulated by his pursuit of the next rung up the ladder and, as always, the competition for the job. He was downright aggravated by the presence of his competitor in a space that was too small for Phillip alone, so he decided pacing wall-to-wall would provide some minor physical relief and allow him to concentrate on what he wanted to tell the board if it did call him back in. And it was not a minor factor in Phillip's decision that the pacing would make it easier to ignore the old guy almost moaning in pleasure as he wiggled in the leather chair.

"Geez, this chair is nice. I wish I had this one at home. It'd be perfect for watching hoops. Kentucky versus Duke, cold beer, and, let's see, maybe warm corned beef on rye. That's where this chair belongs."

Huh? They're deciding our futures in there and you want to talk about how to keep your butt comfortable watching basketball? I wish the board could hear you now. They'd let you take that chair home to finish your retirement.

Phillip chafed in waiting rooms. He didn't like to wait for anything. If you're waiting, he figured, you're not doing. And if you're not doing when you're a salesman, you're not selling and you're not making money. He didn't even like waiting in line at the grocery store on a Sunday morning because there was always something next on his list of things that had to be done, whether it was restructuring a corporate sales division or edging the side of his driveway after the grass was mowed. Time waiting, to Phillip, was time that could be spent making something happen.

Ben hadn't risen through management because of his pretty face. He started at the bottom of his profession and worked his way up because he could sell, not just products and services, but ideas. With as many decades in the profession as he had, there were so many experiences sitting in waiting rooms that he might well be in contention for the world record for time spent waiting—lifetime category—if he had documented it all for Guinness. He'd come to grips with that particular aspect of his chosen field of endeavor and long ago learned the time waiting could be spent pacing and building frustration or it could be spent enjoying whatever the circumstances allowed. For Delaney, that usually meant a pleasant experience whenever he had some company with a willing ear. Phillip's ear wasn't exactly willing, but the size of the room meant he was close enough to satisfy Ben's waiting room entertainment purposes. Besides, Ben didn't always talk just to talk. Usually he talked because he had something to say.

"You like seafood?" Ben began.

Phillip stopped mid-pace and turned toward Ben with the look of a man whose thought process had been irritatingly interrupted. "What?"

"Do you like seafood? Because tonight I'm going to have some of the best fresh shrimp and grouper to ever touch a taste bud. You like seafood?"

"Yeah, Mr. Delaney, I like seafood."

The way he said his name sounded, at least to Ben, a lot like passive-aggressive politeness, which was exactly what Phillip had intended.

And with that, Phillip's pacing began again. *Geez, I wish he'd shut the heck up. Where was…oh, yeah, if I get called back in I've got to tell them what I'll do about—"*

"My friend Bill invited me to dinner tonight."

Come on, Ben, I don't know about you, but I'm in the middle of a job interview here.

"He's going to bake some of the grouper and deep-fry some, too. He's such a good cook I can never decide which I like best. 'Course, that just means he'll have to cook for me again, to help me make up my mind." Ben looked out at the same view afforded by the company's CSO office and wondered as he spoke how anybody got any work done with that daily distraction.

Phillip wondered what the heck Ben was looking at as he spoke.

"It's Bill Travis. You know Bill?"

Phillip didn't know him personally, but he knew about that guy because he was in the local paper a lot. They were the same age, and, like Phillip, Bill Travis was rapidly moving up the ascending side of a high-reaching and possibly limitless career arch. Travis was already chairman of the Board of County Commissioners. He was well known in the area, but Phillip didn't actually know him. Now, to figure out which of the yes-or-no answers would pacify Ben the quickest and keep him quiet the longest.

"I know about Bill Travis." *Shoot, wrong choice,* Phillip thought immediately when Ben's eyes lit up like he'd seen the camera's red light turn bright and it was time for the performance to begin.

"I've known Bill since before he was in high school, when he worked for his dad who was one of my customers. Good kid. I never saw him wait around to be told what needed to be done. He finished something and then looked around for what else needed to be done. I thought he was gonna take over the family business."

Maybe his dad still needs help. If you're looking for work, why don't you start there? Phillip's pacing continued without slowing, just like the pace of Ben's story didn't slow just because his captive and reluctant audience refused to.

"He was in high school when we started this seafood dinner tradition. His daddy had a boat, and the three of us went fishing. Netted enough shrimp for bait and dinner, then caught a really nice grouper, in the forty-pound range. But that was about twenty years ago, and he might have started out in the twenty-pound range the first time I told this story."

Come on, Ben. Right there! Seven people are right there behind that door deciding the future of my career. I don't want to hear stories about you lying about how big a fish was. Just shut up, would you, and let me think? Immediately Phillip got the answer to his unspoken question as Ben's story continued.

"Funny thing, Bill was the cook even back then. Good, too. Says his momma showed him how to make seafood taste better than God intended. He has a recipe for tartar sauce that I would consider dying for. It's that good. He's worked years perfecting it," Ben said as he leaned back in his chair and took a deep breath. "For a while there, we missed our dinners together. Politicians are always busy, either working on getting elected or working on getting re-elected. But Bill's got a little more time since the wife and kids left for good. One of the few benefits of being alone is he can take the boat out like yesterday. Says it's nice being out on the water and away from everything for a little while. Grouper and shrimp, too, same as the first time we went fishing together. That's why he called and invited me over tonight. I'm tellin' you, I wish his dad were still around to be there with us.

"You said you like seafood. Want me to call Bill and see if there's enough for one more?"

"No, uh, thanks. I'm gonna have dinner with my family, Mr. Delaney," Phillip answered, because it was easier than telling the truth, that he'd have dinner at his office as was often the case. He'd catch up on what didn't get done while he was interviewing for a new office, then been forced to wait and listen to fish stories.

"Too bad, Phillip, and this is kind of a small space to be using last names, don't you think? It's Ben, I'm sure you know. Anyway, Bill's a politician, but when he's not after your vote he's actually a pretty decent guy. Easiest thing to do is tell him you're gonna go to the polls just to vote for him on election day, then he gets a little less political. When he's not being a politician, like over a fish dinner, you'd probably like him. You guys have a lot in common. He likes to pace, too."

Phillip's stride slowed, and it was just enough to be noticeable, like the smile on his face, neither of which slipped past Ben though he was still looking toward the window.

There were probably people—no, there were *definitely* people, and probably lots of them—who'd argue the point, but Phillip did actually have a sense of humor. It's just that it made rare and short appearances, and by the time Ben had taken note, Phillip's smile had disappeared and his pacing was back to its previous speed.

"You know, that boy wanted to be a politician even then. Did every-thing right, too. Good grades, good college, joined local political groups right out of school and started putting together his net-work. Did you know when he got elected to town council he was the youngest elected official in the state? Just twenty-four. Maybe twenty-five, I forget."

I did hear something about him being really young.

"Yeah, and four years later he became one of the youngest mayors in state history. When he ran for county commission chairman, he was already experienced and knew what it takes to get elected. Let me tell you, in election years, he's a campaigning son of a gun, too. First time running for county office and he gets almost 70 percent of the vote. Geez, I wish I had him on my sales staff. Anybody who can get 70 percent of the votes can sell anything."

Phillip tried another look of exasperation directed Ben's way, but the older man just kept talking as if the two were sipping coffee at the counter of Dunkin' Donuts instead of locked in competition over a job they both wanted.

"Bill's got two kids, just like you," said Ben, making sure his storytelling pace kept astride Phillips pacing. "I haven't seen 'em in three or four years now. I think they're living in Louisiana with their mother. That's where she was from."

Even though Ben didn't need ESP to sense Phillip's disinterest and mounting impatience, the story continued. "I know the price I'll pay for tonight's meal, though," he said with sigh. "Bill's not as happy with the life of a politician as he thought he'd be. Seems he may have lost some of his mojo with the public, too. While I'm savoring each morsel of grouper and shrimp, I'll be hearing about how him being chairman doesn't mean the other board members support or respect him. Wanna know how good his tartar sauce is? I'm willing to listen to that while I eat."

Good God! I'm trying to think here. Is he too dense to figure out I'm not listening to a word he is saying? I don't have time to hear about what someone's paying in aggravation for a meal. I've about had enough of this garbage.

"He'll be complaining about how he'd spent years convincing his friends from the private sector to leave their companies and help him change government. Good people. Capable people. And yet they're all failing. Blah, blah, blah. He'll probably be whining about how hard it is to get anything accomplished in government, while his email and PO box both overflow with hate mail from his constituents, who are impossible to satisfy and never shy about letting him know what they're dissatisfied with now. And all that while I'm spooning tartar sauce. Personally, I'm thinking he's looking down the road at the next election and realizing there's a decent chance it probably ain't gonna happen. I hope all that talk about politics doesn't ruin my appetite."

Phillip stopped dead in his tracks. "Did I just hear you say something about tartar sauce and losing your appetite? Honestly?" The words left his lips as a plea. "Ben, no disrespect intended. I've heard you're a storyteller. I get it. But, frankly, I haven't even been listening to most of what you've said. I've got way too much on my mind to think about politics, seafood, and condiments. For God's sake, please, Ben, can you just give me a moment?"

The older man's eyes were surrounded by wrinkles, but they were bright and clear and locked on Phillip's as he spoke.

"I'm trying to give you a very important moment, my friend, but it appears you're not interested. Maybe one thing you haven't heard about me is that I never waste a story. I wouldn't tell one if there was no purpose in it being told. And you have no idea how hard it was for me to do it without holding a cigar."

You must be joking. Fishing, dinner, politics, and a cigar? This keeps getting better and better.

"That story had nothing to do with my desire to share my dinner plans, Phillip. I was telling it just for you and just for this moment in your life. And frankly, the message would have been quite boring and you wouldn't have listened anyway if it had been delivered any other way. You can thank me later, if you'd like."

At that moment, something happened. The frenzy of thoughts racing through Phillip's mind that had been focused on the new job and the board, suddenly left its intended target and turned to an attempt to piece together a conversation in which he only remembered fragments like "baked and fried," "70 percent of the vote," "private sector," "shrimp," "constituents," and "tartar sauce." *Tartar sauce? Was there a message hidden somewhere in there? Just For him? Really?*

Phillip's pacing had stopped and his head was cocked slightly to the right when Ben concluded with, "I have a strong feeling if we ever meet again, you're going to want to pay a lot more attention."

Phillip's impatience demanded a quick explanation and the missing moral to the story. He wasn't in the mood for games in business, ever, and even less today of all days. He expected the quick, direct answer he wanted, or at least was ready to demand it when the door to the waiting room reopened.

In stepped Chairman Bergman followed by the six other board members, each of whom shook the hands of Phillip and Ben as they thanked them for their interest, participation in the interview, and waiting afterward. Phillip didn't want to waste a second of the invaluable time he had left with board members, but he also didn't want Ben leaving without giving him the punch line the old man insisted lay tucked away somewhere in the story. As Phillip continued politicking with his parting words of excitement that reemphasized his desire for the CSO position and how perfect a match he would be for the company, he couldn't help but look over his shoulder to measure Ben's location relative to the door. Phillip broke away from his own conversation, raced to the door at a rate a little faster than he'd been pacing about the room earlier, and tapped Ben on the shoulder.

"Got a minute?"

Now Phillip was ready to talk. What a difference a few minutes and a hanging point make.

"Before you go, tell me the point of your story. Just give it to me. It's not that big a deal. I'm just curious."

"No, my friend," Ben said with a knowing wink. "Seafood and tartar sauce await, and my buddy Bill says he's actually looking forward to some of my stories. Remember, I never waste an opportunity, especially when I have a cigar and a willing ear."

Ben continued speaking, just a little louder with each step as he headed down the hall toward the elevators and away from Phillip. Without even turning, his words echoed back down the corridor.

"And no matter what happens with this gig, you ever find your ear is willing, don't hesitate to call, Phillip." Ben stepped into the waiting elevator, and as the door was about to close, his head poked out for some parting words. "As a matter of fact, if the position turns out to be yours, call me a few months in, and I'll tell you that fish and tartar sauce story again. By then, I imagine you'll find the end and my point a whole lot more interesting."

And with that, the elevator doors closed like a curtain dropping to close a performance, and Ben was gone.

Phillip mumbled to himself, "This old guy is screwing with me," and stepped back into the waiting room for the last round of smiles and handshakes. He didn't know it then, but by the time he returned, his fate was sealed. The journey to transformation had begun for Phillip, the soon-to-be-appointed CSO, and the sales organization he was to lead. And it certainly wouldn't be last time Phil would hear Ben tell a story. By the time it was all over, Phil would be able to write a book...

CHAPTER 3

The Next Big Thing

Arguments for both candidates were strong, but on paper and in person, the two couldn't be more different. They were both successful men—that was where similarity began and ended.

Phillip knew the industry, the technology, and the market. He was currently working at a company that served as a perfect example of the level of success the organization interviewing him wanted to achieve. Though relatively young, his drive and enthusiasm had won over at least the spirit of most of the board members. His presentation was clearly focused on hiring the right people to achieve sales transformation, and that pleased everyone.

A new breed of salespeople, a hybrid mix of one-part technologist and a bigger-part problem solver, wrapped in the heart and spirit of a hunter, would drive greater sales and customer relationships. He used the performance of his current sales organization as evidence of what could be accomplished under a Phillip Evan Hawthorne regime. He would hit the ground running and dare the rest of the organization to catch up and keep up with him. And the board members had to notice his energy level. Once he stood to talk, his rear end never creased the seat of his chair again. He showed purpose, conviction, and a confidence they had to realize verified Phillip's every claim without a hint of doubt.

Ben hadn't walked in ill prepared. He'd done his research on the industry, the current technology and trends, in addition to the overall market, but he had no experience or direct connection with any of it and wouldn't hesitate to mention that during the interview. His background was in publishing, and while he'd always been fascinated with technology, he had never thought about selling it. Contrary to his younger competitor, Ben's tush remained firmly and comfortably planted in his boardroom chair, his only motion a gentle rocking as if he were telling stories on a front porch with a cold glass of sweet iced tea in his hand. He had captivated the board with his quiet confidence and his ability to connect as if he had known them all since they'd been kids playing baseball until it was too dark to see the next pitch coming toward the plate.

He admitted he had never transformed a sales organization and wasn't even quite certain why there was all this fuss about "sales transformation." As far as he knew, the principles for selling the right way, effectively managing a sales organization, and developing long-lasting customer relationships had been and always would be, well, the same. Nothing had to be "transformed," he told the room full of company directors. If anything, it just needed to be redirected to the right track. Ben had been successful in convincing the board he was very much like the members themselves, like he was one of them, and that would figure prominently in the board's decision about who should become the new leader their company's sales efforts.

It was funny. Did opposites really attract? The board's decision would certainly appear to support that long-repeated notion. Everyone looked for things in others they admired, but didn't personally possess. In this instance, that resulted in two things. One, the board felt Ben possessed too many characteristics they and their senior management already had. While wisdom and maturity were both admirable qualities, there was no shortage of either already among the company's assets. The board and company wouldn't lack either if it decided to allow Ben to gently slip back to retirement. Phillip represented a new level of spirit and enthusiasm, new blood, a fresh start. But second, and more importantly, there was something else Phillip possessed that his soon-to-be employer didn't. When it came right down to it, it was not "the opposite" that attracted the board—what was attractive was something as yet unresolved or even mentioned.

As it turned out, the biggest moment in either interview came as an answer to a simple question posed by Board Chairman Bergman. She wasn't necessarily looking for one of those magical bonding of opposites, but something the candidates may have that this organization didn't, something major.

"We don't want to be seen as poachers," the chairman said as her eyes locked onto Phillip's to make sure the CSO candidate could not mistake the gravity of what was to follow, "but is there the possibility of you bringing along some of your top performers to sell and help you manage your team here?"

This was a nugget of information the CSO candidate found surprisingly difficult to hold in until the right moment. That moment had arrived. The Cheshire-cat grin on Phillip's face amply demonstrated that he'd been waiting to share an answer he knew the board would like.

"I thought you would never ask. Ms. Chairman, you don't want your company to be seen as a poacher, and I don't want to be seen as a thief. Some of the top performers have no-compete provisions in their employment agreements, but a lot of them don't. And if we provide the right opportunity and financial incentive, I wouldn't have to steal anyone. There most likely would be a line forming to follow me here."

Phillip glanced around the room at each face and saw that his dramatic presentation of the team he could put together was very effective. Everyone received it with thoughtful looks punctuated by slight nods. Later on, when Chairman Bergman posed the same question to Ben, that candidate's response would ultimately doom his attempt to end his unwanted retirement and return to the active workforce.

"As you know, Ben, your competition for this position is currently employed by one of our fiercest competitors. That means we have the possibility of some of the industry's top sales and sales management talent following him here. As a matter of fact, he seems pretty certain they will. Any possibility of you bringing some of your top performers with you?"

While Phillip could hardly wait for that question before answering it, Ben's reaction again pointed out to the board that they were very different people with very different ideas being interviewed, not two candidates spouting the same campaign slogans.

Ben leaned back in his chair, his chin resting casually in the palm of his right hand and said, "Hannah, while I'm certain my people could sell anything to anyone, they are all quite happy where they are. At my age I don't think I have the physical strength to wrestle them to the ground and drag them away, and that's about the only way they would come with me. Or go anywhere else, for that matter. I may have created the environment in which they could succeed, but I certainly didn't have the power to take it away from them when I left. The process and structure are firmly in place. At this moment, they are where they have the greatest chance to succeed.

"The good news is I don't have any problem working with the folks you've already got. I've inherited more than one group of someone else's people, and for the most part it's always worked out pretty well. It's all about giving them the process and structure they need to succeed."

And there it was—the single biggest factor that determined who would be the new chief sales officer.

In a five-to-two vote, the board of directors made the final decision. It would be Phillip Evan Hawthorne, CSO. He brought youth, enthusiasm, and new ideas. Ah, but the real golden prize was the prospect of attracting sales and management talent from one of the industry's top competitors—seasoned pros with long-term customer relationships and a history of production. With just one strategic move, board members may have not only replaced a failed CSO, but also acquired all the sales and management talent needed to truly transform the organization.

It had all the appearances of a great decision.

As Phillip had speculated in his interview, a line of sales and management talent did, in fact, form to follow him, and it formed quickly. An expensive line, too. It turned out the talent from Phillip's previous employer didn't require the kind of physical force Ben had said it would take for his people to come aboard. For Phillip's people it was the gravitational pull of money, and lots of it.

With all eyes on the human resources required for transformation, there was no hesitation by the board to approve Phillip's request for higher base salary levels and richer incentive programs for the sales organization. It was no different from playing the free agency game in sports. Sometimes you got an opportunity to buy a championship and sometimes you got what you paid for. Sure, the free agency game was a gamble, but less of one when the talent was old enough to have proven their ability to produce but still young enough to keep improving. Given the previous performance of Phillip's team of people, there was little doubt of a payoff.

Sixty days into Phillip's tenure, he announced the majority of his team was in place. By then, a full 25 percent of the sales and sales management team he inherited had been churned. They were replaced with either top performers from his previous organization or the most successful salespeople from the industry sector's other major players who had been lured by the lofty and highly publicized sales incentive packages being offered. It seemed everyone who was anyone wanted to play for this team. Everyone liked to play for a winner, and this company was surely going to be one.

Everyone was in a hurry but understood how things worked and knew some patience was required. Phillip and the board were all experienced enough to understand buyers' decision cycles, and that dramatic changes wouldn't happen immediately just because a new nameplate adorned a tenth-floor office door. Even with an all-star free-agent lineup, it would take at least a couple of quarters before anyone would expect to see significant upward movement in revenue. But that time had come and gone, and Phillip's own patience was being tested by the calendar. Results weren't expected immediately, but really, by the end of the third quarter? C'mon, this was Phillip Evan Hawthorne, and it would have surely shown by then.

Nope, not even by then. As a matter of fact, at the nine-month anniversary of Phillip's appointment as CSO, results were as flat as a flour tortilla and just about as exciting. The high-priced, free-agent sales talent he had recruited to transform sales seemed to have transformed themselves into the same lackluster sales team the company had before they were signed. They had done nothing more than drive sales expenses to new and lofty heights by not only cashing the checks for their higher salaries, but also demanding even greater investments in engineering, marketing, and administrative support.

In less than three days, Phillip faced a board review of sales performance in the same room where his interview had been conducted and the offer to become chief sales officer had been extended. He'd have to muster the same passion and enthusiasm that landed him this coveted position and convince the board members more time was needed for his team to build confidence in the company and its offerings.

From the beginning, the board had made commitments to give Phillip and his team everything they needed to successfully transform the company's sales organization and, most importantly, produce results. Board members saw the investment the way a concert promoter sees the rider on a rock star's contract. Van Halen's contract rider had once stipulated: "There will be no brown M&M's in the backstage area, upon pain of forfeiture of the show, with full compensation." The board of directors wasn't exactly picking all the brown M&M's out of the bag by hand, but it was willing to go to extra lengths to make sure Phillip, who was hired to be the company's own rock star, and his band of salespeople were happy performers.

Even with all the pampering and extra attention the stars received, "We're not in Kansas anymore," became a phrase shared all too commonly among them. They had long ago begun to appreciate more and more the environment of their former company that included a stable and dedicated customer base and the resulting stream of steady, recurring revenue. Team morale also suffered under the realization that the new recruits missed being the face of the industry's standard of excellence and nothing less. Sure, they'd joined the new team as hunters, but soon found out the prey for their previous organization had been bred for them as buyers, cultivated with the idea that biggest and oldest also meant best. Fear of change caused many of their old customers to buy whatever their previous company was selling because, well, they always had.

The free agents were shocked, just like the board of directors and the new CSO they'd hired, to find out the customers who had trusted them so much before would not follow them to the new company like they had all followed Phillip. A few of the older account executives had already returned with their tails between their legs to the safety of their previous employer. Many who stayed were questioning the wisdom of their decision, especially on payday. While the new base salaries were very impressive, without the fat commission checks they were all used to taking home, their incomes wouldn't come close to matching last year's W-2's.

In the break room, some had even begun to wonder aloud about Phillip's future as chief sales officer.

Phillip Evan Hawthorne was deep in thought, contemplating what metrics he could possibly pull out to show any positive trend for sales performance. Proposal activity was up. That was a good thing. Phillip had demanded each account executive keep the revenue equivalent of four times their quota in their sales pipeline, so the proposal mill was always churning. Unfortunately, closing ratios had dropped enough to offset that increase. And while they were generating more activity, the dollar value of the average proposal had also dropped, which meant the sales staff was finding fewer opportunities to sell the depth and breadth of their new company's product and service portfolio. The best salespeople he knew had followed him here, but 80 percent of his sales were still being generated by just 20 percent of his people. And, even more confounding, most of those who were hitting or exceeding their numbers weren't the people he'd brought with him.

Phillip found himself staring out of his tenth-floor window at nothing in particular, just as David Malone had done a year before.

How could this be? This company had almost everything in place to achieve transformation: good products and services, a robust sales force automation system, decent marketing programs, aggressive pricing. All they needed were the people, and I put together the dream team. Did the higher salaries make them lazy, or are they not quite as good as I thought they were?

Just as Phillip reluctantly closed the last of his incomplete spreadsheets to call it a night, these words came through his slightly opened door, almost as if in a dream: "You like seafood?"

His tired eyes opened as his head jerked left toward the heavy, wooden office door to his office. He hadn't thought about Ben Delaney since the elevator doors ended their conversation following their day of interviews and waiting together. But suddenly he expected to see Ben's face poking through a door again.

"Whoa, Phillip, you look like you just saw an IRS agent."

Back to reality, Phillip saw Geoffrey Roberts, one of his regional sales directors, instead of Ben Delaney. Déjà vu was one thing, hallucinations quite another. With all the pressure he was under and the toll of less and less sleep as the months progressed, it wouldn't have been surprising if his sleep-deprived brain conjured up visions of Ben or anything else. But this time the voice was real.

"Oh, sorry, Geoff," Phillip finally responded. "You just caught me off guard and the way you asked the question reminded me of something I hadn't thought about in a while. That's all. Yeah, man, I love seafood. Why?"

"A friend of mine took his boat out yesterday. Caught a good-sized grouper and netted some huge shrimp. He is a cookin' machine. Bakes a little, fries a little. Makes his own tartar sauce. Some of the best seafood I've eaten. He's invited a few friends and—"

"Stop!" Phillip held his hands out and frantically looked around the room for video cameras. Was he being punked? "You must be joking. Don't tell me. He used to fish with his dad. He's in politics. County commission chairman. Could it be Bill Travis?"

"Okay, now you're freaking *me* out, Phillip. What the heck? How did you know? Do you know Bill? Don't tell me you've eaten his seafood." Geoffrey took a seat on the arm of the leather chair by Phillip's door. He had a huge smile plastered on his face.

"No, Geoff. But I gotta say this guy must be one heck of a cook. I've only talked to one other person who knows him, and you both said almost exactly the same thing in the same way." Phillip's head was instantly flooded with the memory of how irritated he was the last time he'd heard about Bill Travis's culinary skills. *Am I a jerk, or what?*

"I've only heard one fish story about Bill. And I never really quite got to the end of it." With that statement, something pressed the little right arrow "play" button in his mind, and he clearly heard Ben Delaney say,

"As a matter of fact, if the position turns out to be yours, call me a few months in and I'll tell you that fish story again. By then, I imagine you'll find the end and my point a whole lot more interesting."

Phillip left-clicked his mouse as if it would stop Ben's voice from playing and looked at his darkened computer monitor as if a program were still running.

"Just curious, Geoff. You know who else will be there?"

"I never know, Phil. Always characters, though. Always stories. Always fun. You coming or not?" Geoffrey stood, looked at his watch, and twirled his car keys on his right index finger.

"I think I have to, or I think I'm supposed to, or something. But yeah, I'll follow. A good story or two might be good right about now. As a matter of fact, it may be just what I need."

And with a stroll to the same elevator that Ben had ridden back to retirement, a swipe of his parking card at the garage gate, a call to his wife about his change in plans, and a left turn up the ramp to Interstate 95, Phillip Evan Hawthorne, CSO, took the next step in his journey to sales transformation.

CHAPTER 4

It's Not a People Problem

Phillip's drive up I-95 was slowed by those pesky afternoon "pop-up" thunderstorms cooked up by hours of oppressive heat. You were always told to stay off the roadways in the South when there was even a hint of snow or ice because Southerners were "steering challenged" when driving in even the mildest of winter conditions. Evidently, they were equally challenged when water wasn't in a solid state. Southern US roads were filled with native drivers who began losing control of their vehicles somewhere between the first raindrops and when it was time to turn the windshield wipers on. Maybe they didn't teach rain in driver's ed. Whatever the cause of the regional affliction, it slowed Phillip down. Another fender bender presented itself every few mile markers and true "rubberneckers" couldn't care less about the severity of the accident. While puddles of blood among horrific wreckage may have been preferable, puddles of mud and a dent would suffice for those who had to see what there was to see.

Despite conditions that would test his patience on his most patient of days, Phillip actually enjoyed the time, including the stop-and-go part when the difference between stop and go was barely noticeable for a few miles. Being alone in his car provided him with the kind of quiet and solitude he needed and wanted but couldn't seem to force into his already-hectic routine. Right at his finger-tips he had hundreds of satellite radio options; a CD player with a nearby case that contained some of the finest music ever recorded, including his normal Interstate sing-along favorites "Hotel California" and "Cocaine;" plus the auxiliary input for his iPod. So he sure wasn't lacking for choices to keep his mind occupied with something besides gridlocked traffic and sales numbers. But for once all the modern substitutions for original thought remained unused during his time behind the wheel. For Phillip Hawthorne, this was a time for reflection, introspection, retrospection, and letting his mind wander free in search for new thoughts, new ideas.

As he followed Geoff up the highway, Phillip mused to himself about what a difference three quarters could make. Who would've thought he'd be driving through a rain-soaked rush hour hoping he would see Ben Delaney at a fish fry in the backyard of a person Phillip had never met? Today, he found himself as anxious to hear what Ben Delaney had to say as he had been to shut him up just nine months before. Who knew, Ben might be nothing more than a weaver of stories for entertainment purposes only. Given Phillip's current state of mind, that might not be a bad thing. But Phillip suspected there was more. He would only admit it to himself, but he really hoped there was something to learn from Ben.

The shower stopped just as Phillip followed Geoff around the final turn. The street had turned into a parking lot in front of the surprisingly modest home of County Commission Chairman Bill Travis. Phillip looked for a space that would allow for an unencumbered, speedy exit and wondered how quickly and gracefully he could eat and leave if Ben Delaney wasn't there. He sure didn't want to endure a combination of stories about fish and politics—two things he always felt were one and the same.

As he smiled and joined Geoff for the walk up the driveway to the front door, Phillip realized how foolish he was to have gone through all of that trouble for the sole purpose of "running into" Ben Delaney. It would have been so much easier to Google Ben, get his phone number and call him, as Ben had suggested nine months before.

But no, that would've been far too overt. Phillip's ego wouldn't allow him to admit he was actively seeking advice from Ben, or anyone else for that matter. He wanted his reintroduction to Ben to appear coincidental, unintentional. *"What a surprise to see you here. Who would have thought?"* The question would be whether or not he could surreptitiously lure Ben to a spot where they would have privacy. Even then, he would have to find a way to coax information from Ben without giving him the impression he wanted or needed it.

As it turned out, his reintroduction to Ben was anything but coincidental and unintentional. It was Ben who "out-coverted" Phillip. It was he who'd arranged for the young CSO to be invited that night. Ben had met Geoffrey Roberts at Bill Travis's home several fish fries before. He was fully aware that the company's "sales transformation" hadn't gone as Phillip or his board of directors had envisioned. He knew the sales team Phillip had brought on board wasn't performing as expected. He'd heard stories of how unhappy most were and that some were even leaving. And Benjamin Delaney wasn't at all surprised.

Ben hadn't been stalking Phillip, just observing from a distance. He knew Phillip's ego would prevent any contact between the two of them, so he had kept in casual contact with the two members of the board who cast their votes in Ben's favor. And that wasn't in an effort to weasel his way back into contention for the CSO position if Phillip failed. It was because he really wanted Phillip and the company to succeed. Ben loved to see organizations turned around, made right.

The still-retired Ben was quite pleased when, at one of Travis's regular seafood cookouts, he found the person sharing the bowl rapidly filling with shrimp shells worked for Phillip as a sales director. Geoff Roberts was equally surprised he was sharing a shell bowl with someone who, had things gone a little differently in an interview, could have been his boss. *What a small and interconnected world we live in.*

Ben had marked his calendar for the final day of Phillip's third quarter as CSO and, if Ben hadn't heard from him first, he had every intention of calling Phillip on that date. Nine months was the gestation period for a human baby, so it was certainly a long enough period of time for Ben's fish-and-tartar-sauce story to develop into something meaningful for Phillip. At least Ben hoped so.

Ben positioned the surprise as a "reunion" of the two CSO candidates and asked that no one tell Phillip of the charade. The seafood dinner consisted of grouper and shrimp Ben had "caught" and paid for at the seafood market less than a mile from Bill's house. He had arranged for Geoff and the CSO's administrative assistant to make certain Phillip's calendar was open and to make sure the plan went off without a hitch.

Ben had even prepared Geoffrey for the invitation—just the right words, tone, and inflection to jar Phillip's memory when he heard, "Do you like seafood?" and the description of what was being baked and fried that night. He had prepared Phillip's sales director for a harder sell, but Ben suspected the extra effort wouldn't be necessary. And it wasn't.

In deference to the high likelihood that Phillip would bring his ego to dinner with him that night, Ben planned for privacy, placing two chairs and a small table in the far corner of Bill's backyard. He and Phillip would be separated from the grill and large picnic tables where most everyone congregated by a small group of Sago palms, a row of lit Tiki torches, and the entire length of Bill's kidney-shaped pool.

Geoff didn't knock. He let out what was evidently his signature "whoop" as he passed through the open door. Before anyone actually saw him, a chorus of "Geoffer-man!!!!" echoed from the kitchen and through the sliding-glass doors that led to the grill and pool. As Phil followed Geoff toward the kitchen, introductions were coming at him far too fast for him to even attempt to attach a name to a face. An ice-cold Miller in a bottle, snuggly wrapped in an Atlanta Braves koozie and clearly still the champagne of bottled beers at Bill's famous fish fries, was firmly planted in Phillip's left hand before he had time to refuse it.

If aroma was any indication, Bill Travis was, in fact, every bit the culinary master at least two people claimed he was. Cajun spices combined with the unmistakable scent of onions, sweet peppers, and garlic sautéing in real butter. *Okay.* Phillip inhaled deeply and smiled. *It's not going to kill me if it turns out Ben isn't here.*

County Commission Chairman Bill Travis was in charge of things here, too, standing in the kitchen over a massive bamboo cutting board, filling a bowl with what appeared to be finely chopped pickles, cabbage, and peppers. He had someone over each of his shoulders, both asking questions about ingredients, measurements, and servings. A large jar of homemade mayo was nearby. *Was he making tartar sauce?* It appeared so, and as soon as he realized it, Phillip didn't even try to stifle his loud chuckle. He remembered tartar sauce being a part of Ben's truncated story. *Was there a message hidden somewhere in there? Just for him? Really?*

As Phillip and Geoff approached, Bill held up both of his latex glove-covered hands and said, "Sorry, fellas, no handshakes or hugs. I am deeply engaged in practice for my career after politics. I miss one pepper or pickle, one little bit of cabbage, and I start over. Don't want to be rude, but the gang here has pretty high expectations for my tartar sauce and, more importantly, they are all future customers when it hits grocery store shelves one day. Who's your friend here, Geoff?"

"This is Phillip Hawthorne, Bill." Bill slapped Geoff's hand with a wooden spoon as Geoff tried to take the last pickle from the cutting board.

"Ouch, Bill. It's one pickle, for heaven's sake. Give me a break, I'm hungry."

"Good to meet you, Phillip. And, Geoff, you want the tartar sauce to taste the same as it always does every time you eat here? Then don't touch the ingredients." Bill was holding the wooden spoon over the pickle daring Geoff to try again. Then Bill pointed the spoon at Phillip. "Hey, wait a minute. Phillip Hawthorne? Aren't you the guy who helped my good buddy Ben Delaney stay retired?"

"First," Phillip began his response with a smile, "I must say I've never seen anyone so fiercely defend a pickle. And, yes, Ben and I were both considered for the same job. I just got lucky, I guess. At least some days I feel that way. Ben was a great competitor and a very interesting character. I wish I'd gotten to know him better, but I was a little too preoccupied with the interview to let that happen."

"Well, congratulations on the job, Phillip." Then Bill rested both gloved hands on the edge of the kitchen counter and leaned toward his first-time guest. "And for your information, I wasn't defending the pickle, I was defending the process by which I produce the best tartar sauce that ever graced a bite of seafood. It's a science. It's exact. And it works.

"Actually, my friend Ben has been counseling me on it for months. I've been working on him to join me when I incorporate *Chairman Bill's Famous Tartar Sauce.* As a matter of fact, I should thank you for keeping him available for me."

Bill went back to dicing the nearly poached and final pickle.

"As for getting to know Ben Delaney better, you should have that opportunity tonight. He's out in the backyard smoking a cigar and working up an appetite." Bill grabbed the wooden spoon and raised it, then waved it toward the door. "Just go out through here and past the grill. Follow the Tiki torches all the way down the pool. You'll find Ben just beyond the palm trees."

"Thanks, Bill. And this is the first time I've been more excited to taste tartar sauce than the fish I'm putting it on."

Phillip stepped through the sliding glass doors and down the three brick steps to Chairman Bill's backyard. While the house itself was modest, Bill had created a tropical paradise in his sizable backyard. He had a top-of-the-line Viking stainless smoker and grill, a little Tiki bar that looked as if it were modeled after the original in Islamorada, twinkling white lights in the palm trees, and a great sound system over which reggae music played. *Nice groove for a politician.*

Phillip paused for a moment and surveyed the pool and backyard. His eyes followed the torches to the stand of palm trees on the other end of the yard. Through a space between fronds, he saw the red, burning ember of a lit cigar. *Ben's beacon.* He wondered as he walked along the edge of the pool and closer to the wafting cigar smoke if Ben would already have a story in progress, even if he were alone. If Phillip were really lucky, maybe it would be the finish to the fish story. Phillip could listen surreptitiously from behind the palms, get the punch line, and leave by the side gate of Bill's backyard.

No such luck. As Phillip stepped on the first of a dozen or so footstones leading around the Sagos, Ben bellowed, "Who goes there?"

Phillip hoped the foliage guarded him well enough so Ben didn't see him jump. At that moment, Phil realized he was a little more nervous and apprehensive than he'd thought.

"Well hello, Mr. Delaney, uh, I mean Ben. We are still on a first name basis, right?"

"Well if it isn't Mr. Phillip Evan Hawthorne, CSO. What a pleasant surprise! How are you, my friend? Pull up a chair!" Ben waved his cigar at the only other seat that side of the pool.

"I'm doing well, Ben. And you, sir?" Phillip was surprised at how lively and animated Ben was during his greeting. It really appeared as if Ben were glad to see him. He reached out to Ben's extended right hand and accepted a hearty handshake.

"Okay, Phil. I'm doing quite well, actually." Ben remained seated as he reached for the arm of the chair next to him and turned it slightly toward Phillip. "I see you couldn't get through the house with out a cold one. No one can. How about a cigar?"

"No thanks, Ben. Never been a smoker. My dad enjoyed a good cigar and the smell brings back great memories, so don't worry about me." Phillip grabbed the back of the chair and swung it around to the other side of the table directly facing Ben.

"Me neither, Phillip. I call myself a non-smoker. I know I'm delusional, but I can't bring myself to accept that a cigar is really smoking. I mean I know it's on fire and I can clearly see smoke rising from both ends of it, but if I thought of it as smoking, I'd have to quit. It's more of a social thing for me, that and it's a really good timer." Ben reached out for the ashtray fashioned from a coconut shell at the center of the small table and gently used its edge to shave off a quarter inch of ashes from his cigar.

"A timer. What do you mean 'a timer?'" Phil smiled, leaned back, and wondered if he should tell Ben his cigar was also a backyard beacon.

"Well, my friend, I know you know I'm a bit of a story teller. Some say I could go on spinning tales all night, and they're probably right. An old and dear friend taught me to use my cigar as a gauge. When it gets to where I can't hold it any longer, it likely means people listening to me can no longer hold whatever I'm saying." Ben examined the cigar as he held it in front of him and turned it slowly between his fingers. "So you know, I do stretch it as far as I can. The longest cigars are called 'Gran Coronas' followed by 'Presidentes.' Most times you'll see me with a Gran Corona, rarely less than a Presidente."

Phillip looked at Ben's cigar, surely a Gran Corona, and wondered if there was enough left to get to the end of the fish story. He imagined Ben snubbing the last of his smoke and walking away again before the moral of the story could be delivered. *Please, not again.*

"Anyway," Ben said as if he had read Phillip's mind, "there's plenty of this stogie left for you to get what you came for."

Wow, that's pretty egotistical. He cocked his head and gave Ben one of those half-smiles he always felt coming on when the rational right side of his brain was doing battle with the more emotional left side. "And what makes you think you know what I came here for?"

A small cloud of smoke escaped Ben's mouth, and he watched it rise toward the cloudless summer sky.

"Well, if our last meeting is any indication, I suspect you might find me a little irritating, not your style," Ben said with a little half-smile of his own, delivered with his eyes locked onto Phillip's to make sure he knew his own had been recognized by the older man. "Yet you've been at this shindig less than five minutes, walked right past a table of appetizers that all would go great with the cold beer you're holding. And you ignored about a dozen really cool guys, all of them more likely for you to hang with socially than with me, and yet you end up in a far corner of Bill Travis's backyard sitting at this table.

"All that didn't happen without you making it happen. You're here for a reason. We both know what it is, Phil."

It had been a long time, before high school actually, since anyone had called him "Phil" instead of Phillip without an immediate correction. This time he didn't feel like his manhood had been assaulted, so he just rested both elbows on the arms of his chair, extending both hands out to each side, palms upward, as if to admit guilt.

"Okay, Ben, you got me. I can't stand things that are unresolved. You left me hanging, man," Phillip said with a slight, almost embarrassed chuckle. "It's true. I was so caught up in the interview process, I just didn't get it and it's bugging me."

"You would've gotten it if we had been there a little longer, Phil. Unfortunately, telling stories takes a little more time than blurting out some unsolicited and unwanted advice. Worth the time and effort, though, as far as I'm concerned.

"Hey, Phil," Ben said, again sounding more friendly than insulting, "it brought you back here, didn't it? Not a chance you'd have come to see me had I not left you hanging, right?"

Ben finished his question with another sacred puff of smoke offered to the sky, while Phil began his answer raising his brew in recognition of the older man's wisdom and experience.

"True once again, sir."

"The good news is I want to tell you the story as bad as you want to hear it because it'll help me prove some of my theories about this idea everyone calls sales transformation," Ben said, leaving Phil wondering just how fish dinners and tartar sauce related to transforming sales organizations.

"You're right there in the middle of it, so maybe I'll be able to help you out a little. In turn, you can help an old man validate his thoughts. Small price to pay, if you're up to it."

"I'm ready when you are," Phillip said as he settled in his chair.

As Phillip leaned back, Ben leaned forward.

"I don't know about you, but during my interviews, I heard the words 'sales transformation' more than a few times from C-level executives and board members. I gotta admit I'd never heard the term before. You?" Ben asked as he pointed his finger toward Phillip.

"Oh, yeah. It's the hot topic right now for sales organizations. Everybody's talking about it. It's hard to escape." To Phillip, Ben's lack of awareness was an immediate reminder of why Ben wasn't right for the CSO position.

"I don't want to sound like an idiot, but do you have any idea what it means?" Ben asked as he rested his chin on his hand.

"You know, Ben, if you ask ten different people, you'll probably get ten different definitions. The long and short of it is, most companies feel they're doing everything they can to streamline operations and cut expenses to maintain or grow profits. When they get to the end of that rope, they have to turn to sales. They realize the only way to improve performance is to make their sales organizations more effective, efficient and productive. So for some companies, sales transformation may be new sales force automation or customer relationship management software. For others it may be new hiring profiles and compensation programs. For some it may be firing salespeople who aren't performing and bringing in new blood. It could be a combination of any or all of those. It just depends on who you ask. "

"That's what I don't get, Phil. I've been selling and managing sales organizations for many, many years and I don't ever remember a time when I wasn't trying to make my teams more effective, efficient and productive. What's new?"

"Good question," Phillip replied. "I think it starts with the fact that the Internet has created a new breed of buyers. They know a whole lot more about their options before they even talk to a sales rep. And you have new competitors popping up all the time. It's getting harder and harder to differentiate products and services. To buyers, I think everything begins to look like a commodity. Price becomes the determining factor for lots of folks, so margins start to slip."

"So the race to sales transformation begins, right?" Ben asked as he leaned back in his chair.

"Exactly. Just like my new company, everybody's trying to put together the best teams and programs. It's just finding the right combination of people, products and services."

Ben picked up his cigar and stared for a moment at its glowing red ember. "And you're telling me this is the hot topic right now. Does that mean just about every company is either planning on transforming sales or already in the midst of it?"

"It sure looks that way, Ben. Certainly everyone in my sector's doing it. It's survival." Phillip found himself staring at the cigar's ember as Ben placed it back on the table.

Ben leaned forward toward Phillip again and said, "Well, now I'm curious. If everybody's doing it, how many companies do you know of that have actually transformed?"

Phillip opened his mouth but no sound came out. He looked to his left at the Sago palms as if it were possible one of them had the answer, then slowly turned his head back toward Ben. "It's funny, but I honestly don't know of any."

"I was afraid of that," Ben said as he reached for his cigar. "You know, Phil, Plato taught that the beginning of wisdom is the definition of terms. If nobody has come up with one definition for sales transformation, how would anyone know when they've accomplished it?"

"You're just full of good questions tonight, Mr. Delaney, but I would suspect it would be when revenue and margins start to grow."

"I may see it a little differently, Phillip. Sales and margin growth may look good on a quarterly report, but unless it's sustainable and long-term, it doesn't mean anything has transformed. That's where I think the definition of sales transformation has to be clear.

"All the problems you describe are created because of the customer's perception of your relationship with them. Like you said, they look on the Internet and see a boatload of choices, all of which

46

look pretty much the same. They see your reps presenting solutions that all look pretty much the same. All, if not most, of the companies they could buy from are qualified, but none of them have any true, sustainable, competitive edge."

"So what are you telling me, Ben? Do we continue to dump money in to research and development hoping to find the next big thing? Our previous CSO convinced the board to do that and, for all I know, he's somewhere standing in a soup line tonight."

"You guys will always invest in R&D, Phil. So will your competitors. But, longer term, it won't matter to any of you unless your customers perceive their relationship with you in a different way. That's what sales transformation really is. It's when you transition your company from being just another qualified vendor to a trusted advisor to your customers. It's when they believe you're a long-term, strategic partner, an asset with significant impact on what they're trying to accomplish as a business."

As Phillip stared off toward the pool, deep in thought, Ben took a quick look to see how much time he had left for the story, according to his cigar. He was satisfied enough to kick off his flip-flops, prop his feet up on the table and get comfortable.

"You see, Phil, if you don't make that transition, you're always going to be a victim of the problems you described. Customers can go from qualified vendor to qualified vendor, find the lowest price for comparable products and services, switching providers any time they want. On the other hand, it would extremely difficult and painful for them to lose a trusted advisor and partner."

Phillip placed his elbows on his knees and put his face in his hands. Through the opening between his palms, he said, "Oh, man. You are so right, Ben. We are definitely in the qualified vendor category right now, and that's exactly why we're not getting anywhere."

"Ah, but I hope that's about to change," Ben said with a satisfied smile. "You know, good 'ol Webster has spent a significant amount of time and energy defining words, and personally I don't think any of us business folk should try to change 'em. If you look up transformation, Webster defines it as 'a change in form, appearance, nature or character.' So in sales, it'd be a change in the nature of how sellers engage customers, managers coach sellers and leaders manage the sales function with the objective of becoming a trusted partner and advisor to the customer. Make sense?"

"Absolutely. What you're saying is true. It's right on. We've got to be a better partner to our customers." Phillip slid his hands from his face to his temples and began to rub. "But I'm still struggling with something, Ben."

"And what would that be?"

"I'm going back to our time in the waiting room at the interviews. What the heck does any of this have to do with fish fries and tartar sauce? It's killing me. And that cigar's not getting any shorter, so you better start talking to me, Ben."

Like any good storyteller, Ben appreciated an anxious audience. And he, too, was a little concerned about his tobacco timer. So he placed his cigar across the corner of the table and, to make sure it didn't roll around, pressed it down gently with his right index finger.

"I'm gonna let this sit for a minute to give us a little extra time. Okay, Phil, let's talk about this journey to sales transformation," Ben said as he leaned forward toward the young CSO.

"I'll start with how I came to choose the story I told you that day," the older gentleman began as the younger listened intently. "I can assure you none of the board members shared anything with me about your interview, at least not until the very end of my conversation with them. And what they did tell me just happened to remind me of my dinner plans for the evening. "

"Do tell." Phillip leaned forward, placing his elbows on his thighs.

"You see, Phil, in simple terms, businesses leaders are responsible for managing three things: people, process, and structure. All three of them are critical—all three are important and all three have to be managed well. So when I ask managers to tell me which they believe is the highest management priority, the vast majority chooses…well, wait a minute, I'll just ask you.

"Suppose, Phil, you take over a new business, or shoot, maybe you even start one. Of people, process, and structure, what's your first priority?"

Pop quizzes in school had never been much of a problem for Phil, but this was different. He wanted to get this answer right for this teacher. After leaning forward to listen, he shifted again, leaning back and placing both hands of the top of his head as if that helped him think. A couple of seconds later, he began.

"Okay, let's see. First, I think you're right, we have to manage all three well." Phillip's hands slid from the top of his head to the back of his neck. "Of the three, though, I think I'd choose people, Ben. I can't do everything myself. I need talent to manage. I need good people to drive the business. People will change the perception of the customer, therefore people will drive sales transformation."

Ben picked up his cigar and then placed it back down on its same corner spot without raising it to his lips. He looked at Phillip with a smile.

"Oh man, I wish I offered to bet on your answer. I'd be collecting my winnings right now.

"Almost everyone I ask chooses the same," Ben explained. "'Our people are our most important resource,' they say, and I understand their position. I get that structure and process are irrelevant without good people to implement. The funny thing is, I believe that opinion creates a huge barrier for this thing everyone is calling sales transformation.

"I think a bunch of sales leaders come to the conclusion that they have a sales 'people' problem," Ben continued. "They believe they hired the wrong people for the job and, as a result, think sales transformation begins with replacing a lot of their sales team. They have too many technologists, not enough business people; too many farmers, not enough hunters. So they churn the bottom quarter or so of their sales team—heck, a lot more in some cases—trying to find the right fit and right mix, only to end up with the same disappointing sales performance they had before.

"The truth is, it's not just a people problem."

Ben carefully shaved a bit more ash from his cigar and took three quick puffs, as Phillip watched closely and tried to measure the distance between the cigar's red ember and the end of Ben's story. While the younger man watched the three small spheres of smoke rise beyond the tops of the palm trees in Bill Travis's backyard, he contemplated what he had just heard.

"Then what is it, Ben? And I still don't get how it's connected to seafood and tartar sauce."

"Just the tartar sauce, Phil, just the tartar sauce." Ben placed his cigar back in its resting place. "Since you entered through Bill's front door and came out through the sliding glass doors to the backyard, you had to pass through Bill's kitchen, right?"

Phillip nodded.

"And if you passed through the kitchen, you undoubtedly came across Bill bent over a large cutting board with a few bowls, knives, peppers, cabbage, pickles, and the like. And if you or anyone else tried to sneak a bite of anything on that counter, I would suspect the back of a hand felt the sting of wooden spoon."

Phil smiled. "Yeah, that's right. I suspect Geoff's hand still has an imprint."

"Well, Bill has good reason. If you hung around that kitchen for more than thirty seconds, I'm sure Bill started telling you about the soon-to-be-incorporated 'Chairman Bill's Famous Tartar Sauce.' Politicians can't stop campaigning, and Bill's already started campaigning for his new condiment business," Ben added with a wry smile.

"Bill has been perfecting that sauce for years with exactly the right spices and fresh ingredients cut and mixed in exactly the right way. He understands that in order to take it to market, it has to be right and it has to be consistent.

"Now he has to figure out how to mass produce his condiment goldmine and keep its level of quality to where you, the grocery store consumer, feel you're being served his sauce straight from Chairman Bill's kitchen counter, save for the whack of a wooden spoon. That's a tall order, my friend," Bill said to his attentive one-man audience.

"So now Bill starts his business and, like I said, has three things to manage: people, process, and structure. So what do you think Bill should do first? What's his top priority? You think he should go out and try to find master tartar sauce makers? The best in the business? Set 'em loose with knives, cutting boards, mayo, and veggies? Probably not," he answered his own question. "Bill has to make certain he clearly defines the *process* by which he produces consistently excellent tartar sauce first. Then he can take ordinary people, 'cause I hear tell master tartar sauce makers are extremely hard to find, teach them his process, and produce extraordinary results."

Ben was pleased to see Phil almost imperceptibly nodding along in agreement as the tartar sauce story continued.

"If you examine any department of any business that produces consistent results over a period of months, years, or even decades, it is typically because someone has identified the logical, repeatable process by which the department performs its function. It doesn't matter what people in the department come and go. It doesn't matter who is on vacation. The processes implemented and managed by the business are what drive the performance. Accounting, inventory control, human resources, shipping/delivery, dispatch, R&D, and manufacturing are, in all successful businesses, driven by a clearly defined process."

"You see, Phil, without a clearly defined process, Bill could take good, capable, well-meaning people, leave them to figure out how to make tartar sauce on their own, and set them up to be victims of failure. Then all he could do is blame *them* for producing bad sauce."

Phil had been so intent on paying attention to Ben's words that he had forgotten to check the timing of the cigar.

"The sales profession is a weird animal, Phil. A lot of people think it's a 'people' profession and selling is an innate skill, that there are born salespeople. You find someone with an outgoing personality and a little aggression as character traits, give them some product knowledge, and send them out to hunt.

"Most sales managers don't care, except for moral or ethical concerns, how their people sell as long as they produce," Ben told Phil. "As a result, most companies just try to find the best salespeople they can. They don't believe it's a process problem. As a result, the vast majority allow their salespeople to use random or informal selling processes, which basically means whatever the salesperson or sales management feels is right at the time. The idea is 'They are salespeople. They should know how to sell. They should do whatever has worked for them in the past.'

"And here's the awful shame of it, Phil. Some senior company leaders cover their own butts by blaming the salespeople for the crappy performance."

Ben picked up his cigar again but decided the timer was working fine and gently set it down again. As he leaned back to continue his story that hadn't mentioned fish fries and tartar sauce for quite a while, the still-new chief sales officer leaned forward. He didn't want to miss anything. Not now.

"So, during my interview with the board of directors the day we met," Ben said, "the chairman tells me it's possible you'd be able to bring some salespeople with you, like they were some kind of prize. Not a word about you bringing a process," Ben said. "My first thought was 'uh-oh'."

He saw Phillip twitch at hearing that.

"Think about it, Phil. The people who were working at the company you were hired to transform came from the very same talent pool as the team you brought with you from your old company. If they weren't performing up to expectations, it likely wasn't just a people problem. It's much, much more likely they hadn't been given the process to succeed.

"And as far as you bringing in new talent? That guaranteed a transformation, all right. You transformed the people you brought with you into the same mediocre sales performers you already had on board when you took over. Unfortunately, if you pit a competent sales person against flawed process and structure, flawed process and structure will win every time."

Luckily, Ben paused to pick up his cigar for what had to be some of the last draws. That gave Phil time to slow down his racing mind. He looked up at the night sky, and as clear as the stars he saw the truth.

What Ben said is right. Every bit of it's right on the money. His top performers from the old company hadn't been successful because the organization had provided a clearly defined sales process. It was just their environment—a lucky one to be in. They sold for the industry leader; most had been there forever and had long-time relationships with their customers. They were order-takers, not salespeople. *Look at them now. They aren't performing because they're lost. And, geez, Ben's right. I'm blaming them for it. Wow.*

Phillip brought his gaze back down just as Ben was putting what was left of his cigar back on the table. "So you believe sales transformation begins with defining the process by which your entire sales team sells. Are you telling me the entire sales team should be selling in the same way? Is that correct? Shoot, is that even possible?"

"Absolutely, Phil. As you'll see, for many reasons, it's not an easy task, but I would strongly encourage you to invest the time and effort to make it happen. I don't think you'll achieve sales transformation without doing it. To change the customer's perception, you've got to change the way your sales people engage them. If you want better, longer-lasting relationships with your customers, you better be able to show everyone how to do it.

"And unless you have a process of your own, you'll have to find a partner that has one that you and your entire team believe in. And you've got to own the process, just like Chairman Bill in there," Ben said with a nod of his head toward the kitchen, "owns the process for making his tartar sauce, and you need to protect it with your own wooden spoon."

Ben sat straight up to say, "Phil, the process has to be science, not art. It's got to be learned knowledge and applied skill, not something innate."

Ben leaned forward and tried to lock eyes with Phillip, but that wasn't to happen. His young audience leaned his head back to stare up at, well, what appeared to Ben to be absolutely nothing. That was fine. Ben's cigar and the first of what would be many lessons for Phillip Hawthorne were complete. Finally, the connection between a fish fry, tartar sauce, and sales transformation had been made.

As Ben gently pressed his cigar on the bottom of the coconut ashtray to end its short but productive life as the timer of his story, Geoff Roberts walked through the middle of the Sago palms.

"You boys hungry? Bill's laid it out and if you're not quick, there'll be nothing left."

"Starving," Ben and Phil said in unison.

Ben rose from his chair, and the three men headed toward the awaiting tartar sauce and some fish that had somehow become the condiment in that night's meal. As they walked, Ben placed his left hand on Geoff's shoulder.

"How's your daughter, Geoff? Still teaching her how to drive?"

"Oh, heck yeah, Ben. That girl scares me to death. I sit in the passenger seat a nervous wreck. Sometimes I wonder how I made it back home without having to change my drawers. I'm barking orders the entire time. Hands are at ten and two. Hands are not on your mobile phone, not in your purse, and not on your lip-gloss. It never stops."

Ben skipped back to the small table and reached down to the stub of his cigar, by then only about the size of the end of his thumb. He picked it up, and held it toward the light of the closest Tiki lamp.

"I can't stand to waste fine tobacco or good stories, and it appears I have a little of both left, Geoff." With that, Ben reached into his pocket to grab his lighter and simultaneously reached into his vault of stories, firing up one about his father teaching him to drive.

Come on, Ben. Couldn't you have used the last of that cigar to help me a little more with people, process and structure? Phillip ended up walking a few steps ahead as Ben and Geoff strolled to the pace of a story about Ben's dad and how Ben had learned to drive in his father's beautiful 1965 Mustang. *Thank heavens this story is for Geoff.* Phillip had enough to digest from one of Ben's stories and lot more important things on his mind as he thought about returning to work, maybe even tonight.

Phillip's knee-jerk response of "I'm starving" was an exaggeration. He may have been hungry, but wasn't really sure. His stomach felt uneasy at best. All he could do was think about the possibility he had let his company down by focusing on getting the right people and not implementing the right processes to help them succeed. A master chef didn't just hire good cooks and let them loose in his kitchen. How could he have missed something so important, and so obvious?

The first-time chief sales officer had been so certain that the people he brought on board were all he needed to transform the sales organization and fix his new company's problems. So far he had not only failed his employers and their shareholders, but also the new team he'd brought with him. And there were the people he'd inherited. He had probably let down some of the sales reps and managers he had let go as he purged a quarter of the sales staff, too.

As he walked toward Bill Travis's overflowing picnic tables slightly ahead of Ben and Geoff, Phillip couldn't help but overhear bits and pieces of Ben's story about learning how to drive. Just like Ben's seafood story in the waiting room after the board interviews, Phillip caught a word or two between his own thoughts: "compliance," "prisons and military," "exercise machine," and "babies and car seats." *Man, could this guy get wrapped up. What could any of this stuff mean to Geoff if he was trying to teach his daughter to drive?* Well, that was for Geoff to figure out. Phillip was now certain it was all connected to something meaningful, or Ben wouldn't be wasting the last of his cigar. Right now, though, he couldn't even begin to try and figure out Geoff's story. Phillip's mental plate was as full as his dinner plate was about to be. Besides, he could get the Cliffs-Notes from Geoff later.

Everything smelled delicious and looked even better, so Phillip fixed a huge plate, sat down at the picnic table, and quickly took a bite of grouper covered in Chairman Bill's tartar sauce. For the first time in his life, he was acutely aware that the flavor of what he was eating was not the result of the innate skills of a masterful cook. That glorious sensation caressing his taste buds came from a clearly defined process that had been developed over time. He had eaten at some of the finest restaurants in the world, many earning multiple Michelin stars. Phillip had never once thought they'd won the awards because they had identified the process and structure by which people other than an award-winning chef could cook for and serve two hundred people a night. The guy with his name on the expensive marquee certainly wasn't in the kitchen seven nights a week making sauces. He wasn't cutting his fingers slicing pickles anymore, but now Phillip could picture the award-winning chef holding a wooden spoon and making sure his award-winning process continued without flaw.

He had a new perspective on sales, too, because Phillip had always viewed selling just like he looked at cooking, as an art created by individuals. Sure, there were some people who were sales artists and successful, but there weren't enough of them in the whole industry to transform his entire sales organization. And there was something else he realized with another bite of tartar sauce on grouper. When a sales artist left, the company was screwed. Artists couldn't be replicated. Successful processes could.

He had long ago gotten over the thrill of arriving at an office with his name over Chief Sales Officer on the nameplate of the door. But tonight changed that. At this moment, at least, thinking about going to work was exciting, like back when it was new. He couldn't wait to get to his office and work with his management team to lay out a plan. They were going to develop a process, a clearly defined sales process for his organization. Just like a master chef running a restaurant, Phillip felt an obligation to show everyone who carried a quota how to be successful with the ingredients they had to work with. Now all he had to do was convince the board it was a necessary next step for the company's sales transformation.

Phillip ate as quickly as he was thinking. He realized just how lost in thought he was when, from the other side of the table, he heard Ben continuing his story for Geoff.

"So, she will drive with her hands at ten and two when you're not in the car only when she believes it's in her best interest, not before. Survival is the strongest of human instinct and …

"Ouch! Dang it! I let this one go too far…man, that hurts."

What was no longer recognizable as a cigar appeared to have fused to Ben's thumb. He ungraciously scraped it on the edge of the picnic table, and when it fell to the ground, Ben grounded it with his foot as if it were being punished for ending his story.

"Anyway, Geoff, you get the point. Now if you wouldn't mind, hand me one of those plates, please. The stogie and I are done storytelling for the night."

Phillip had gotten what he had come for: food for thought with an added bonus of some for his body. He didn't have to think about engaging in any more conversations or hearing more stories, from Ben or anyone else. There was no more talk. The feast County Commission Chairman Bill Travis had prepared took control of everyone there.

For Phillip, it was the right time to enjoy the solitude of the ride home and the beginning of preparation for his upcoming presentation to the board.

"Well, gentlemen, it's been both fun and filling, and I hate to eat and crawl," Phillip moaned as he patted his stomach and arose from the picnic bench, "but I have a huge presentation for work in three days and lots to do in preparation."

Phillip looked down at a still-seated Ben as he stacked his napkins, Miller bottle, and plastic utensils on his oversized paper plate for disposal. "And Ben, what a pleasure it was to listen to your stories tonight. I can safely say I wish I had been more patient at our first meeting. Tonight has been very enlightening. You've given me lots to think about."

The bench was pushed so tightly against the picnic table, Ben could do no more than half-stand, but that still allowed enough flexibility and reach for him to extend his right hand across the table to Phillip.

"My pleasure, Phil. Yeah, I thought you would appreciate my ramblings a little more now. And you'll find that last little story every bit as important as the one about tartar sauce. You won't believe how critical it will be for you to understand motivation," Ben said, giving Phillip a knowing wink. "If you have any questions about it, I sent you an email earlier this evening with my mobile number. Don't hesitate to use it."

Phillip grabbed Ben's hand, nodded, and winked back while at the same time trying to think of what "last little story" Ben could be talking about. *Oh, no. Wait a minute.* The only time Phillip heard the word "motivation" was during Ben's story for Geoff about learning to drive. *The driving story was for me and I wasn't paying attention? Really? Prisons? Exercise machines? Car seats?*

Phillip couldn't admit he hadn't been paying close enough attention to know what "last little story" Ben was referencing, so he released the handshake with a smile, then dumped his plate into the trashcan at the sliding glass doors and found Bill Travis by the grill to thank him for the fabulous meal. Then he turned toward the fish fry crowd and gave a sweeping wave and a loud "See ya, guys!" to everyone gathered.

Phillip's lack of interest in the beauty of a classic American automobile only meant that later on he'd wish he had paid attention. As he exited through Bill's side gate, though, he couldn't shake the feeling that Ben's story about learning to drive in his father's Mustang had been the beginning of his next lesson on sales transformation.

CHAPTER 5

Hands at Ten and Two or How to Motivate a Sales Team

The next two days would be a blur for Phillip. There was no doubt that on the third day Phillip's board would be pouring through pages of numbers as they questioned the progress of the company's sales transformation and sales results. Phillip's presentation would show increased proposal activity, as well as a minor, positive blip in topline sales numbers for the previous quarter, but certainly not what he or the board had hoped for or expected at Phillip's three-quarter mark.

He wasn't ashamed of the job he had done nor would he try to hide from it. He couldn't. It was what it was. It is always difficult when the introduction of new leadership resulted in people losing their jobs, and ramping up a new sales team was expensive and time-consuming.

It was clear to Phillip that he had used all of the runway he could to put his sales staff in place. The first nine months would be positioned in his report to the board as a period of purge and setup as Phillip put the right team in place for transformation. No, the results hadn't been spectacular—flat would be the appropriate description—but the churn of the bottom of their sales force hadn't hurt them, either. Unfortunately, even with his previous employer's top sales performers on board for almost all of the last nine months, 80 percent of the company's sales were still being generated by the same 20 percent of the sales organization that was in place and producing when Phillip took over as chief sales officer.

The focus now had to be what to do with all his high-priced talent. Phillip's presentation wouldn't be about his first three quarters as CSO. Phillip wasn't one to dwell on the past anyway. It would be year two and beyond for Team Hawthorne. Going forward, it would be all about sales process.

Phillip did, though, have one small problem. No budget had been requested or approved for a project of the magnitude he suspected implementation of a universal sales process would be. There was a sale to be made, and probably the most important sale of Phillip's career. And to make it, he had to convince the board of what Phillip himself had once thought not true: that selling was a logical, repeatable business process. That it was science, not art. It was not just about the best people. It was about providing the best sales process possible for *all* of your people.

Phillip was certain Ben wouldn't mind if he borrowed, word for word, from the lessons shared in Bill's backyard. As a matter of fact, he was certain that was exactly what Ben wanted. As a result, Phillip had committed most of it to memory on his way home from the fish fry. Yes, he knew from Ben's wisdom that sales process should have come before he had his team in place, but unless Ben had told them otherwise, the board probably wouldn't know.

And the seven members of the board of directors didn't. Phillip used Ben's "People, Process, Structure" question and, true to what Ben had said through a small cloud of cigar smoke just three nights ago, all but one board member chose people as the top priority. Just like Ben, Phillip wished he had made a wager.

Phillip agreed with the board majority on the *importance* of people. He had to, given the fact he had made getting his team in place his number-one priority the day he took over as CSO. The way he looked at it, he had little choice but to put people before process in this particular case. If people were going to come with him, the sooner they did, the better. Okay, maybe that wasn't the real reason Phillip didn't make process the highest priority, but it must have sounded good to the board. They unanimously approved the idea and the budget it required.

The clincher in Phillip's presentation to the board had been pure Benjamin Delaney: "Unfortunately, if you pit a competent sales person against flawed process and structure, flawed process and structure will prevail every time." This newly discovered (at least to him) "truth" about sales transformation would become the topic of the remainder of Phillip's presentation and the cornerstone for his new sales plan. Nine months was a reasonable amount of time to put the right team in place and ramp them up on an extensive product and service portfolio. Now was the time to take it to the next level.

Not one of them said a word, but Phillip also knew the board members were likely to lay blame for the flawed process on David Malone, the previous CSO. Malone had tried more than one sales training initiative, each failing to produce any positive outcome. But he had never suggested implementing a company-wide, singular, universal sales process. To the board, this idea was something they'd never tried before. It was the kind of new, progressive thinking they expected when they'd chosen Phillip Evan Hawthorne over Ben Delaney as the new chief sales officer.

And it only proved how intoxicated the board was with the "people" aspect of Phillip's hire. Not one of them remembered Ben talking about the challenges of creating and changing process and structure when considering the transformation of an organization. While everyone could recall Chairman Bergman asking Ben about the prospects of bringing his top people with him, no one remembered his response:

"I may have created the environment in which they could succeed, but I certainly didn't have the power to take it away from them when I left. At this moment, they are where they have the greatest chance to succeed. The process and structure are firmly in place. The good news is I don't have any problem working with the folks you've already got. I've inherited more than one group of some-one else's people and, for the most part, it's always worked out pretty well. It's all about giving them the process and structure they need to succeed."

Just like Phillip, had they only listened more closely the day of the interviews…

Phillip spent the better part of the next three months working with his management, the company's learning organization, and sales operations to develop a clearly defined process for selling. In an effort to get his people involved, too, the entire sales organization was surveyed for input. It was no surprise to find many needed help with prospecting, qualifying customers, and handling objections. There were also requests for help with presentation skills, time management, and account management, all the kind of responses that were expected.

Top sales talent from both Phillip's old organization as well as those he inherited were interviewed. The idea was to figure out what worked for the "best of the best" and replicate that for the rest of the team. Combine that with the learning organization's already-owned "off the shelf" content to close identified gaps from the survey, and sales operations for integration into the sales-force automation system and, in a remarkably short period of time, the program was ready to launch.

Phillip made the decision to pilot two classes prior to rollout. His request to field sales management was to send folks from the bottom 50 percent of the sales organization—the weakest performers.

These were the people who needed help the most and were more likely to get the biggest benefit from the introduction of the process. Even if the process needed major retooling, it certainly wasn't going to hurt them. And if this group didn't see any benefit, it was highly unlikely anyone from the upper 50 percent would either.

The pilot program was greeted with enthusiasm, especially by his lower-producing salespeople who were anxious for the help. Post-course comment sheets were all positive. Yes, a few tweaks were necessary, but overall feedback was good. Phillip was pleased that everything had fallen into place quite nicely. Everyone involved had done his or her job effectively. And finally, with great company fanfare and anticipation, the program was launched to the general sales population.

And it was a dismal failure.

Within sixty days it was obvious something was very wrong. Managers saw little change in the performance of their sales reps. Salespeople claimed the new process was either too much, or not enough. Most saw it as another burden to manage on top of an already overwhelming workload. Even those who did use what they learned used only bits and pieces. Many salespeople who had not gone through the program were reluctant to attend future programs. Some of the classes were less than half full; others just cancelled their training outright. Worse, the company's sales stayed flat.

Phillip couldn't have been more conscious of the importance of producing results from the program. At a cost of $2,000 per head, plus travel and expenses, the CEO and board would have little patience with failure. Nor would Phillip. He'd bet his position as CSO on what he thought was the sound advice of Ben Delaney and the compelling logic of the requirement for logical, repeatable sales process as a gateway to sales transformation.

He hadn't just taken the time to get field level input through the surveys, but on the content of the process. Phillip had even field-tested it to positive reviews. The sales organization, including his new recruits and his legacy salespeople, had asked for help in specific areas of sales knowledge and skill, and the learning organization had delivered. The program was positioned as "the" process by which the company was going to sell, but most salespeople had viewed it as just another "flavor-of-the-month" program—just one more short-lived management fad. "This too shall pass" seemed to be the prevailing sentiment in the sales organization.

Well, failure wasn't an option. He laid down the law to everyone: the process was no longer an option. If he and the board said a universal sales process was a necessary and core element of transforming the sales organization, the people who didn't believe that probably didn't belong in the company any longer. And he let everyone know. Implementing the process was mandatory—that was the order handed down by Phillip to the entire sales organization. No more half-full classes. No more cancellations at all. Everyone attended. Everyone participated.

And yet thirty days later, with half of the staff fully trained, they were still producing the same miserable results, but with a new problem. Morale in the field was horrible.

Salespeople were being forced to attend the training. Those who had attended were forced to provide management with proof of their use of the process through a series of weekly reports. If they wanted to get their commission checks, they had to input information collected through the new process into the sales force automation program. Everyone felt they were being held hostage by the new process. In a way, they were.

After finishing another weekly status call with his management staff that relayed plenty of negative input about the new process, Phillip turned his chair away from his desk and looked out the window. As he admired the magnificent view, his thoughts turned to Ben Delaney.

What is it? What did I miss, Ben? We defined a process. It's good and repeatable. It works universally for the company's sales reps. It's based on science, not the artistry of the salespeople. What is it? C'mon, Ben, what'd I miss this time?

"And you'll find that last little story," Ben's voice came to him as clearly as when they were parting at the fish fry, "every bit as important as the one about the tartar sauce. You won't believe how critical it is for you to understand motivation."

Phillip spun back around to make sure Ben hadn't snuck in behind his back or was waiting just outside. Nope, it was Ben talking to him, but he wasn't really there. And he was right—again. Clearly, the sales staff wasn't motivated to do more work required by a new sales process. They certainly weren't seeing any positive results in their paychecks. Phillip knew the process was good and would work, but he also knew his salespeople didn't think so and didn't like having to implement it. They simply weren't motivated to use it, even when field level management was taking heat from above and then beating them over the head to use it.

Phillip couldn't make a connection to motivation with any part of Ben's story told at the small table in the corner of Bill Travis's backyard. He had listened to Ben intently until the cigar timer had signaled the end of the tartar sauce/process connection. That he got. But motivation? He did remember Ben mentioning that the entire organization had to own the process. Phillip had mandated ownership. The sales staff had no option but to own it, and the withholding of commission checks for failure to use the program was his version of Bill's wooden spoon.

But the last thing that night, the very last thing, was that telling wink from Ben and, "You won't believe how critical it will be for you to understand motivation." *Do I really understand motivation?*

Phillip certainly thought he was motivational. He had always been able to rally his direct reports when faced with obstacles, deadlines, or things like new programs or procedures. He also believed that salespeople, and even managers in some cases, were somewhat like children and, given the right circumstances, should be treated accordingly.

Phillip had a great role model for this type of motivation. A strict father who *believed* he was always right had raised him. While his father admitted that was a potential character flaw, he would say he made up for it by always *being* right. Sometimes, that was the role a father. For sales transformation and the implementation of the sales process, Phillip was the father and chief sales officer. While his sales team may not believe him at the moment, Phillip knew the implementation of a universal process was important. It had to be done his way, just like his father had demanded, because he was right.

Still, it just wasn't working. There had to be something he was missing. Maybe Phillip wasn't the motivator he thought he was. Or maybe his managers weren't motivational. Who knew? Maybe there was more of a story to motivation than he thought there was. If that was the case, Phillip realized, there was probably one person who could tell it.

He pulled out his cell phone to get Ben's number. He rationalized that it would never be needed, but had saved it anyway. And Phillip hated to admit he missed the point of another story and maybe wasted weeks or months on a process that should be working but wasn't. He pressed the call button.

"This is Ben Delaney, how may I help you?" It sounded to Phillip as if Ben were a corporate receptionist or a freshly trained call center rep, except he knew, in this case, the "how may I help you?" wasn't the script, it was sincere. He couldn't help but smile.

"Mr. Delaney, and I call you that with the utmost respect, sir, this is Phillip Hawthorne. How are you today?" Phillip waited for Ben's admonition for calling him Mr. Delaney, but it didn't come as directly as expected.

"As always, *Mister* Hawthorne," (*There we go.* Phillip smiled ever broader). "I'm doing quite well. I've been very busy working with Chairman Bill on his tartar sauce project. Talk about a challenge. Not nearly the challenge that transforming a large sales organization poses, huh? And how goes it with you?"

"We're doing some really good stuff." Phillip was surprised he answered with what sounded more like his motivational speeches than the truth. Things couldn't be going much worse. "Listen, Ben, I took your advice and sold the board on the idea of implementing a formal sales process as the next step in sales transformation. Frankly, the logic behind it makes so much sense that the board and I believe it's the right thing to do. That's the good news, Ben, now here's the bad.

"I'm giving my team the recipe for making tartar sauce, but every time I turn my back, they're each making their own version of it. Nobody is following the instructions. I'm standing over them with my wooden spoon, and they're getting tired of being whacked with it."

Ben let out an audible sigh.

"Yeah, Phil, I was really, really afraid of that. I've thought about calling you a few times, but under the circumstances I've been extremely hesitant to stick my nose in your business. Right now my nose and the rest of me are available for a story, if you're game. I have a cigar in my pocket that's itching to do some double-duty. There's a café with outdoor seating for us non-smokers at the corner of Lonestar and Third with a pretty decent little view of a Little League ball field. It's not close enough for the noise to bother us. Can you meet me there in a half hour?"

"You bet. I know right where it is. I used to play Little League ball at that park," Phillip replied with no hesitation. "And Ben, do me a favor. If you feel the story is longer than a Presidente, either bring two or one slow-burning Gran Corona."

"Oh, Phil, I'd never light two of those precious things for one story, but I'm sure a Presidente will be plenty. See you in thirty minutes, my friend."

With that, Phillip stuck a pad of paper and his laptop into his computer case, even taking a couple of seconds to make sure he had backup pens in working condition because he wasn't missing anything this time, and left for his next story and lesson on sales transformation.

Ben was already there and seated when Phillip arrived at the café. A cigar, an old and battered cigar cutter, a lighter, and an ashtray were positioned on the table as if props for a magician. *How fitting.* Ben was dressed as he was for the fish fry, with the same cargo shorts, bright blue Polo shirt and flip flops. As Phillip approached the table, he removed his jacket and tie. He found himself wishing this were happening at another fish fry in Chairman Bill's backyard.

"Hola, mi amigo, Felipe! Your chair awaits!" Ben used his right foot to push the cushioned, wrought-iron chair away from the table and toward Phillip.

"Thanks, Ben. I can't tell you how much I appreciate you coming here. I'm sure technology seems boring after dealing with condiments, huh?" Phillip suddenly hoped Ben wasn't offended by the comparison and tried to find out with, "Geez, I hope that doesn't offend the chairman and cost me more invitations to his visits to tartar sauce heaven."

"It's all quite the same to me. Publishing, tartar sauce, tech. There are fundamental rules of business that apply to everything. The leap from tartar sauce to tech is no leap at all. There *are* universal truths, my friend." Ben picked up this cigar and carefully clipped the end on a bias. "And if I may light this thing, I can share a few more with you."

Now it was Phillip who felt like the child listening to his father. Just like back in school, Phillip pulled a notepad and pen from his case and sat back in his chair. "Light 'er up, Ben. I'm ready."

"Lesson number one for you, Phil, is that if old Ben Delaney is holding a cigar that still has life in it, it's likely the story he's telling has got life in it, too. No more smoke, no more story. And since most of my stories are connected to business, sticking around to the end of both will never hurt you. You should have gotten this one at Travis's the last time you saw me."

Ben took the first puff of his cigar and settled his gaze on his anxious student.

"So, you can't get the troops fired up, huh? You're challenged with motivating your sales team to participate in your new sales process. Well, Phil, let's see if I can guess what happened post-fish fry through the rollout of your sales process." Ben proceeded to perfectly describe virtually every event Phillip's organization had been through up to and including the near revolt of the sales team over implementation of the sales process. The survey of the sales team, interviews with top performers, involvement of sales operations and the learning organization, the pilots with underperformers, the positive comments, the tweaks, the full rollout, the demand for compliance, the push back from the sales team, and the lack of results.

"Wow, Ben. You got a spy on my staff? Have you been talking to Geoffrey Roberts?" Though Phillip's question was only half-serious and delivered with a smile, he also half-expected that Ben would say yes.

"Nope, Phil. No spies and no conversation with Geoff. What I described happens over and over again in business when leadership doesn't truly understand motivation. There's a whole lot more to it than people think. Many people believe it's an upbeat, energetic 'rah, rah,' 'rally the troops' type of thing. Unfortunately, that stuff can be pretty annoying and wear off real quickly. So a lot more folks believe it's all about the wooden spoon, keeping your troops in line. A 'do it my way or else' philosophy. The problem is, while a wooden spoon may have its place, you have to earn the right to use it." And with that, Ben's lesson began in earnest.

"This is the foundation for the story I told Geoff about learning how to drive. He's having a real challenge motivating his daughter to keep her hands off of her cell phone, out of her purse, and on the steering wheel at ten and two. Some say eight and four now, but I'm old school. It's ten and two for me. Regardless, with all the distractions for drivers nowadays, it's hard to motivate your kid, or anyone for that matter, to keep both hands on the wheel." Ben picked up his cigar and pulled a few seconds off the timer.

"You see, Phil, there are three basic levels of motivation. The first level is compliance. That's when an order is given and failure to obey that order results in a negative consequence. It's the 'do it this way or I'll fire you' method used by a ton of managers. It works extremely well in the military or in prisons—places where the motivator has a significant amount of visibility and control of those he is motivating. In business, compliance motivation has a formidable enemy. It's free will. Most people will exercise their free will and do things they believe are best for them personally. In business, we don't have, nor should we even want to exercise, the power and control of a sergeant or a prison guard. Not unless we're running a sweatshop. So free will creates a problem for business managers who use compliance to motivate. For those managers, as long as they are standing over the shoulders of those they are trying to motivate, the employee will do what is demanded for fear of losing their job. The moment the manager's back is turned, the employee will do what the employee believes is best. You can't stop it."

As Ben paused for a sip of iced tea, Phillip made note of his first revelation. He was managing the sales process implementation by demanding compliance. It was mandatory, and failure to obey resulted in the negative consequence of no commission, or worse, no job. He was absolutely certain Ben was right. When his management staff was watching, salespeople followed the new process. When no one was watching, like during sales calls, presentations, or client negotiations, the salespeople were doing that they'd always done, even if it was contrary to the new sales process.

Ben set down his iced tea and continued, "Once again, compliance motivation does have a place in business, but the right to use it has to be earned. Don't worry, Phil, I'll connect those dots a little later.

"The second level of motivation we'll call identification. It's used successfully every day in TV, radio, and direct mail advertising campaigns. My favorite example is the exercise machines you see advertised on TV infomercials. I love watching 'em. What you see are flashes of an extremely well-developed human body flexing highly-toned muscle while an announcer says in this deep, rich voice: 'This could be your back,' 'This could be your thigh,' 'These could be your arms.' Remember, all this is while you're viewing perfectly developed musculature. The marketers are hoping that you will view this inspiring specimen and say, 'Yeah, that's what I want to look like. That's the body I'm after,' then rush to your phone repeating their 1-800 number so you can be sure to get your order in before the midnight deadline. You ever order one of those contraptions, Phil?" Ben asked as if he had fallen for an ad sometime himself.

"So far," Phillip chuckled, "I've been able to resist the temptation and stick to my gym membership."

"Good thinking, Phil, because unfortunately for the majority who order, it sits and collects cobwebs and dust with the rest of the fitness equipment purchased with the same good intentions.

"You see, the problem with identification as a method of motivation is that it's end-result oriented. When someone sees the model's rippling muscles they identify with the desire to have a body that looks like the one they see on TV. They want the end result. What they don't identify with are the countless hours of incredibly disciplined practice, the sweating, grunting, straining, and all the pain that it takes to get that end result. It's the *process* that leads to the end result that's usually ignored in motivation by identification. Even though more powerful than 'compliance,' identification is still not where we want to be."

Revelation number two hit Phillip. He had tried to use identification as a method of motivation by interviewing the top performers and using their input as an example for those who were under-performing. He desperately wanted everyone on his sales team to identify with the end results generated by his sales elite and perform as they performed. From the popular advertising campaign with basketball great Michael Jordan, "Sell like Mike" was Phillip's idea. But there was only one Michael Jordan, and what the sales staff couldn't identify with, nor replicate, were the years of experience, the discipline, the practice, the trial and error, the wins and losses that had brought the top performers to where they now were. Phillip jotted down another note.

Ben watched quietly until Phillip stopped writing, then continued.

"And that, my friend, brings us to the third and the most powerful level of motivation—internalization. Remember, I said the enemy of compliance motivation is free will, right?"

Phillip's nod kept Ben's story moving.

"Well, Phil, free will is *absolutely the key* to internalization," Ben emphasized. "Your salespeople will always do what's in their best interest, which means you have to prove to them that what you're asking them to do is in their best interest. They should, by their own free will, want to do it. That's the only way for them to be truly motivated.

"I'll tell you the same story I told Geoff about learning to drive. It's the perfect example of internalization." Ben held his cigar between the index and middle fingers of his right hand and flicked its end to get rid of some ash. Both he and Phillip looked at what remained of it in an attempt to gauge how much time was left.

"My dad taught me to drive in a white 1965 Mustang. I'll never forget the experience. To get the full picture, you have to know we lived at the beach in Florida. It was the summer and, as beautiful as the car was, it had no AC. I wanted to be cool while looking cool, so the moment we pulled out of the driveway, I plopped my left arm, real cool-like, out the driver's side window. My dad's wooden spoon was the backside of his left hand, and I felt it immediately. 'Hands at ten and two,' he barked. 'Got it, Dad.' And that's how it went every time I wanted to show off my under-developed bicep to some unsuspecting teenaged girl. The back of my Dad's hand ensured my compliance. So what do you think happened the day I got my license and I took my first drive without dear old Dad?" Ben waited for Phillip's response.

"You showed off that awesome sixteen-year-old gun, didn't you, Ben?" Phillip asked, raising his left elbow and hanging it out an imaginary car window.

"Exactly. I was trying to impress anyone I could. Hey, it was in my best interest, man. There was no option. Sorry, Dad, but in a 1965 Mustang, I had to look cool."

Phil and Ben both nodded in agreement.

"So now I have to fast-forward many years later to one of my life's most incredible events." Ben rested his cigar in the ashtray and leaned back in his chair. "I know you're a father, Phil, so you can relate. It was the birth of my first child, my son. What an amazing, miraculous time. When I was getting ready to bring my baby boy home, I bought the most expensive car seat I could find. I strapped that thing in the backseat of my car and tested it with all of my own body weight, and then I tested it again.

"The drive home was, mile for mile, the most intense of my life. As I drove home with that precious new life in my protection, where do you think my hands were on the steering wheel?"

Phillip held his hands up as if he were the driver. "I am completely with you. Ten and two, no doubt."

Leaning forward, Ben said, "Absolutely. Hey, Dad's backhand wasn't there with me, but my mirrors were perfectly aligned, I stayed under the speed limit, and you can bet your rear end my hands were at ten and two. Dad didn't need to remind me because it was in my best interest now. I had taken ownership of the process, internalized it, and was motivated. That's the way it works, buddy.

"So while you may have gotten accurate input from the sales team on their desire for help in some specific areas of knowledge and skill, your decision on what program to implement as a solution had to be made like a dictator because the buck stops with you. Then what happened was, you turned around to the field sales staff and asked them to implement your dictatorial decision. And if the team responsible for implementation doesn't buy in, doesn't internalize, you're doomed to failure."

Phillip didn't need his notepad to write down "I've been a dictator," but Ben gave him a moment to let the thought settle in until the young CSO had gotten the full effect.

"The funny thing is, Phil, most people believe the training is about the transfer of knowledge and skill. That's what course developers and instructors focus on. That's what's tested for in the classroom and how typically, at least in the short term, the success of course is judged. Then you have the 'smile sheets' collected as end-of-class evaluations with questions like 'Did you like the course?' 'Was the content appropriate?' 'Would you recommend this course to your peers?' Nowhere will you find questions about ownership and internalization."

That's exactly what had happened with Phillip's new training program, right down to the "smile sheets."

"Phil, you can test the knowledge and skill the students acquired in training and get great test results. But if you don't test for ownership of the process, and your students leave without it, those end-of-class test scores will be the only positive results you get."

Okay, so there was the third revelation of the day for Phillip. The sales team hadn't taken ownership. By the time they determined internalization hadn't taken place, it was too late. The negative impact had already occurred.

"So I think I understand it, Ben." Phillip looked down at his notepad. "The first mistake I made was to introduce the process as mandatory. It left me and my managers with no other option but to manage by compliance." Phillip moved his pen down to the second scribble on his pad. "Let's see, the second mistake I made was trying to get my bottom performing salespeople to behave like my top-performing salespeople. I was hoping my weaker reps would identify with the success of my top 20 percent and sell like them, but there's only one Michael Jordan, right? How am I doing so far, Ben?"

"Spot on, Grasshopper," Ben praised, although the cloud of smoke from the cigar seemed oddly out of place with his old movie Shaolin monk imitation. But he smoked freely, puffing like a locomotive. Ben was somewhat certain that the majority of his lesson had been delivered and accepted. It was possible his cigar timer was no longer needed and could now just be enjoyed as a smoke.

Phillip turned to his second page of notes.

"All right, Master," Phillip said, returning Ben's old movie reference, "the last thing I've got is that training is more than transferring knowledge and skill. The transference is meaningless unless people have decided to take ownership and internalize what they learned from the class. I've got to make sure they believe it's in their best self-interest to use what they learned. Did I get everything?"

"I don't know, Phil. Did you?" Ben asked with his head down but eyes up and locked onto Phillip's, immediately giving the younger man the feeling that he was facing another riddle. This time, though, ego and time wouldn't force him to wait for an answer. Phillip gave both pages of his notes another quick glance.

"C'mon, Ben, I don't want to be paranoid and try to look for something that isn't there, but if there is more, let's not waste what's left of your cigar by delaying the inevitable. I'm a different guy now than the one you met on the day of our interviews. Today you have an open and willing audience."

"Yes. I am seeing a kinder, gentler Phil," Ben said with a satisfied smile. "I also clearly see you have checked your ego but can still be aggressive enough to ask for what you want. I like that, too." Ben decided his cigar was still a timer and placed it back in the ashtray.

"Here's where we are. You have a problem for which you came to me for solutions. So you go back to your office armed with two pages of notes about the significance of internalization and ownership. What do you do now? How will you transition from a compliance manager to a leader focused on internalization? What solutions have I given you? How do you get your team to take ownership?

"Those aren't rhetorical questions, mi amigo," Ben concluded, picking up his cigar again and leaning back in his chair to make sure Phillip knew it was his turn to talk. A quick look and Ben decided to smoke a little slower than he'd thought he needed to before.

"Well, as far as the question about ownership goes, I suspect you have to ask for it," Phillip responded matter-of-factly.

"Ah, if it were only that easy." Ben paused to clear his throat and take a sip of iced tea. "It may be time for you to pick up your pen and notepad again, Phil.

"Get this. Transformation of a sales organization only happens when the behaviors of the salespeople in it are changed. So you've tried to change the day-to-day behaviors of your team and probably know herding cats is a breeze in comparison, right?"

"Exactly. I know because I was one of the cats earlier in my career," Phillip said as he quickly thought of training programs he was forced to attend as an account executive. He even shuddered at the thought.

"Phil, companies invest millions in customer relationship management, sales force automation, sales training initiatives, and marketing materials, and then get lower than expected return because none of these expenditures change the behavior of their sales organization. No behavioral change, no improvement in sales performance, no sales transformation. It happens every day."

All the work and money Phillip had put into the new universal sales process and the training it required didn't get results, he realized, because the behavior of his salespeople hadn't really changed. He made another note of that, and Ben once again politely waited for him to stop writing before he continued.

"Here is the challenge: in order for salespeople or managers to behave differently, they have to first decide *for themselves* there is a gap between their current behavior and their desired behavior. An organization deciding there is a need for transformation and asking people to change, or trying to force them to, isn't enough. What leverage does a manager have in that case? Management by compliance becomes the only call. You say, 'We recognized the need to change, spent the money, and developed or bought the programs, so do it or your fired.'"

Again, Ben sounded to Phillip like he'd had a spy in the CSO's office watching everything that had been tried and was, so far, unsuccessful.

"Geez, Phil, I've seen companies set up programs to offer new ideas for salespeople to pick and choose the things they like. But if the audience doesn't think they have a weakness in a particular area, they ignore it. They think sales transformation is a passing fad, a flavor of the month, and they're just waiting for it to pass and the next fad to come along," Ben said, noticing the younger man's eyes light up. "Sorry for rambling."

"That's okay. You're not rambling. It's amazing, Ben. You're right on. One of my managers even said one of his sales reps called the process 'the flavor of the month.' It's just uncanny how accurate you are." All Phillip could do was sit and shake his head in wonder.

"It's just a universal truth, Phil. If you don't expose gaps in their current behavior prior to teaching your salespeople something new, you're gonna end up with the same randomness or informal process they began with. The truth is if you want adults to change, they have to realize there's something for them to learn.

"Look, if you want to be the driving force behind their change, you're going to have to expose the current behaviors that aren't working, that aren't getting them the results they want. Show them what they're doing wrong and the negative impact that it's having, then they'll be open to new ideas about changing their behavior."

"So what are you suggesting, Ben?" he asked after putting down his pen and scratching his chin. "How—and when—does this exposure happen?"

"The way you're doing things, it should happen in the classroom. Get them involved in roleplaying or a Q&A session prior to each major segment in the training program. They can demonstrate their current skill and knowledge and expose gaps in either or both," Ben suggested, but Phillip saw one problem right away.

"I've got some pretty confident people on my sales staff, Ben, but I don't know if their egos can handle being exposed like that in front of everyone."

"Well, Phil," the older cigar enthusiast asked, "what's the company paying you for, stroking the egos of your employees or transforming your sales organization?"

"Good point, Ben. And frankly, I think their egos are strong enough to withstand whatever we throw at them." Phillip picked up his pen again because he could feel Ben was in a storytelling groove. "There's even more to it, isn't there?"

"Where there's still smoke," Ben said waving his cigar, "there's still story. Listen, you can get their attention by showing someone what they're doing inefficiently, but the real change won't happen until your folks are motivated to adopt a new behavior that clearly shows them how to close the gaps in their current approach. Remember internalization?"

Phillip didn't even speak, he just flipped back to the first page of his notes and showed Ben where he'd written INTERNALIZATION in all caps and underlined three times.

"You got it, Phil. Since your folks will do what they believe is in their own best interest, they'll have to believe that a new approach, new systems and materials—the new process—will yield higher sales, more income for them, and greater job satisfaction. That means management and those developing and delivering your programs have a sale to make. Their sale is to have people in the organization use processes, programs and tools for themselves, not because the company demands it. If they can't make that sale to your staff, if your salespeople don't believe in it, trust me, nothing happens."

It sounded easy enough while sipping tea at an outdoor café, but if the question Phillip was about to ask didn't clearly convey his doubt, the expression on his face certainly did. "So how do you do that in the classroom? I can see exposing weaknesses and gaps in behavior, but testing for internalization and ownership? That has to be tough, Ben. How in the heck do you do that?"

"Do you know the meaning of the word axiom?" Ben set his iced tea back on the table and waited for Phillip's response.

"I believe it has something to do with mathematical formulas. Am I close?" Phillip looked to Ben for acceptance of his half-answer.

"Yes, Phil, that's one definition. Mathematicians use it, but for us, the definition of axiom we'll use is 'universally accepted truth.' A mathematical axiom would be a formula that is proven to be, beyond any question, accurate, undeniable. No one could challenge its validity because it is unchallengeable and universally acceptable as truth.

"For you, that means when you develop a process for all of your sales reps to follow, each and every one has to accept the process and its output as an axiom, a universally accepted truth."

Phillip caught Ben glancing at his cigar. "Okay, Ben, so before we go, give me an example of a universal truth for selling."

"You and your sellers can't be just salespeople. You have to become a trusted advisor and partner to your customers. To create that type of relationship, everything your sales folks do has to be in the best interest of your customers. Would you agree that this is universal truth?"

"Absolutely." Phillip couldn't have been more emphatic in his response.

"Then that becomes your test: THE test for each and every segment of your new sales process. Is each step of the process in the customer's best interest?

"That question has to be asked at each stage of the development of your process, Phil. As a matter of fact, take it a step farther. It has to be asked in the classroom, and I mean asked of every single person there. Do you believe that what you are learning supports the customer's best interest better than what you were doing before? If the answer is yes, then it passes the test of truth. You can be more certain of internalization and ownership. If the answer is no, you shouldn't be teaching it anyway."

Ben picked up what was left of his cigar, and Phillip was disappointed to hear the older man announce what was obvious. Their third meeting was about to draw to a close.

"Well, my friend, it's about time for me to go work with the condiment king, Chairman Bill. Before we go, though, I promised I'd connect those dots between internalization and compliance. They actually create a continuum. This is why it's so critical you understand motivation and how internalization and compliance work together."

Phillip had been waiting for this punch line; he grabbed his pen again and was ready to write. "Okay, Ben. Let's do it."

"The intent of implementing your process is to show people how to do the right thing in the right way, to always focus on the best interest of their customers. Well, let's face it, Phil. A lot of salespeople know what's right, but don't always have the self-discipline do it. Sometimes they do the quickest thing or the easiest thing.

"So, here's something really cool. There is an amazing power that comes from getting your sales reps to verbally, in front of you and everyone else, take ownership that your sales process always represents what's best for the customer. The moment they do, you have earned the right to pull out your wooden spoon and manage by compliance. From that point forward, you are only holding them accountable for their commitment to do what they believe to be right and true. C'mon, now, how cool is that?" Ben asked while sporting a smile from ear to ear.

"Very." Everything was making perfect sense to Phillip. He'd lost count of the revelations, but suspected they could no longer be counted on one hand. "I have one final question for you. When can we do this again, Ben?"

Ben smiled, brushed some stray cigar ash from his lap, and tucked his cutter and lighter away in the pocket of his cargo shorts.

"Grab a clean sheet of paper and write down these questions. I'd like you to be able to answer yes to all of them. Right now, I know you couldn't. If you come to a point where any of them stump you, call me. My humidor is full and my calendar isn't, so I'm sure we can find some time."

Phillip had long given up trying to guess where Ben was headed, so he went right along with the command. "Ready when you are, sir."

Ben raised his left hand, spread his fingers, and pointed to each finger as he gave Phillip the questions.

"Number one: Have you clearly defined a formal process by which everyone in your organization sells?

"Two, has every part of your process passed the test of being a universally accepted truth?

"Three, is the process focused on expanding the value you deliver the customers through the sales engagement?

"Number four, have you piloted the process with a broad spectrum of your sales team, not just the underperformers, to make certain it is applicable an accepted by all?

Ben stuck up his left thumb by itself for the next question. "And number five, do all of your salespeople believe the formal sales process will produce significant impact on their own sales, margins, and income?"

For the final two questions, Ben held up the index finger and thumb of his right hand. "Six, is the process dynamic enough to allow for the uniqueness of your customers and changes in your competitive landscape?

"And finally, can your sales process stand the test of time by supporting changes in your product and service portfolio?"

As Phillip finished writing the last of the seven questions, Ben grabbed the check for his iced tea, stood, and headed toward the café door.

"Ben, please at least let me buy your tea." Phillip stood up an extended his right hand for the check.

"No, Phil. It's worth the price of a cigar and a glass of tea to have you help validate this old man's ideas." Ben continued toward the door. Just before reaching it, he stopped and turned. "I'm curious, Phil. When you look at the questions, what do you think you will tackle first?"

For the first time, Phillip thought he was a step ahead of Ben. "Well. I can answer yes to the first question today. We have a formal process. So it seems obvious to me that we need to revisit its contents." Phillip looked down at his notepad. "Let's see if I can read my scribble. My note says that we've got to be certain the process can pass the test of being universally accepted truth. It has to be focused on expanding the value we deliver to our customers through the sales engagement." Phillip looked up at Ben and said with confidence, "That becomes my number-one priority."

"Excellent, Phil." Ben opened the front door to the café and stepped through.

Phillip stared at the door as it closed and all he could do was smile.

As he packed his notepad and pen, the door reopened and Ben's head popped in just as it did through the elevator doors after the CSO interviews.

"One last thing, Phil. Remember, to a man with an ax, everything looks like a tree." The signature Ben Delaney wink and nod followed, and the closing café door acted as the falling curtain on yet another performance.

He simply can't resist, can he?

And Phillip continued his journey to sales transformation.

CHAPTER 6

To a Man with an Ax,
Everything Looks Like a Tree

Phillip Hawthorne was pleased to see that his focus had sharpened and his enthusiasm had recharged in the wake of his café meeting with Ben Delaney. That meeting had only been their third time together, but Phillip was beginning to feel as though he had known Ben his entire life. Unlike their first meeting in the board of directors' waiting room, Ben's stories no longer aggravated Phillip at all. He was actually beginning to consider them a blessing, even divine intervention. Phillip wondered where he would be on the path to sales transformation without Ben's cigars, stories, and guidance.

The older man's advice made perfect sense, too, and Phillip's current challenge was clear. He and his team had to dissect their newly developed sales process and make sure every single element delivered greater value to the company's customers. He couldn't even begin to start answering Ben's other questions with a yes without getting past that first big objective.

Addressing Ben's second question about truth and value had Phillip bringing together the best and brightest from his sales team, learning organization, and marketing department. This time he put them all in one room at the same time. That should be enough brainpower, Phillip thought, to figure out how everything in their process could be in the customers' best interest. It wasn't like they were starting from scratch. Surely a lot of what they had already developed was in the customers' best interest. Unfortunately, when they looked closer, they found they couldn't have been more wrong.

Value to the customers had taken a back seat to the quick sale. The sales process wasn't built around "How do we prove more value?" but "How do we win?" As they went back through each question posed in their sales process, they found the focus was on what the sellers needed to know to make a sale, not what the customers needed to know to make the best decision. Everything in the process had been developed from the seller's perspective; everything was to the seller's benefit. That had to change. Immediately.

The assembled group began to view the process from the buyer's perspective instead of their own, and the challenge became finding ways for their company's technology and service portfolios to actually provide greater value for customers. And it meant Phillip and his people couldn't just bring more value to their customers than before. They would, most importantly, have to prove themselves more valuable than all others in the highly competitive technology sector.

Phillip asked product marketing to present a variety of the company's leading-edge products and services to the group. In turn, the team would brainstorm to find new applications, new ways in which each could be used. There wouldn't be enough time to address each and every feature and function of all products and services, but certainly enough to develop a pattern to apply to all. The search was centered on the team discovering or creating the company's unique differentiators.

"Okay, folks, that's the question right now," Phillip summed it up for them. "What sets us apart from the customer's perspective?"

What followed was a session of complete and utter frustration.

Without fail, every single company feature was greeted with a chorus of "Our competitors can do that, too" from almost everyone in the group. Feature after feature, function after function, and that room full of the company's best sales brainpower couldn't find one single thing their technology could do that some competitor's technology couldn't also do in some way.

So now what?

Then someone in the marketing organization came up with what appeared to be a brilliant idea: "If we're trying to determine what differentiates us from the customer's perspective, why don't we just ask them?"

How simple and logical that was. It was so much so that it momentarily silenced what had been an active, noisy room full of people searching for anything that even resembled simple logic. What made the company different, the differentiators, weren't going to be the same for every customer. Rather than wracking the top brains of the organization, why wouldn't they just put together a presentation of their most powerful technology and services, then go customer to customer to demonstrate it? Right there in the room, with the company's meeting of the minds, the one thing missing was customer input.

Nobody but the customer can decide what's of greatest value to them. Phillip smiled contentedly as he neared the close of another hard, but this time productive, day's work. *I bet ol' Ben would be proud of this.*

The remainder of the team's time together was spent narrowing their broad portfolio of products and services to a set of fifty that represented a unique package. It wasn't that others didn't have some of the same technology; but the complete set was unique. There weren't many competitors, if any, that had the same exact set of features and functions.

Every sales rep would be equipped with a computer slide presentation, script, and glossy handouts. The package would be designed to engage the customer in open conversation about the benefits of technology *specific to that customer's business.* There would be no more guessing at what was important and valuable to the buyer.

The second important decision to come from this sales think tank was to create a group of specialists. They'd be dedicated to specific segments of technology, products, and services. There had been a steady stream of complaints from the field about how much time they were required to spend in training, just to keep up with the company's improvements and changes. It had been taking salespeople's time away from customers and made them resentful of new training sessions, including ones on the new company sales process. With the specialists on board, the sales reps could spend more time with customers and less time in product training. When a specific opportunity was uncovered, the rep could call the specialist in to focus on the details of the features, functions, engineering, and implementation.

It was brilliant. The customers would become engaged and stay involved in the process. They'd see a multitude of Phillip's company's resources dedicated to their account. Customers would definitely see significant value as a result. Yes, it was brilliant. The entire group agreed.

As the meeting began to wind down, everyone was expecting to receive a clear set of marching orders, complete with actions and deliverables with defined objectives and timeframes. This happened at the conclusion of every meeting Chief Sales Officer Phillip Evan Hawthorne had conducted since joining the company.

But it was different this time. Their boss wasn't the type to sleep on decisions, so they were all surprised when Phillip told them that's exactly what he was going to do. In fact, it might be two or three nights, he'd let them know. But for now, they were all thanked for their efforts during the meeting and told to sit tight for a while.

They didn't know it, of course, but going forward depended on free time in the schedule of Ben Delaney. *If only they knew…*

Phillip had made the mistake before of moving forward on a plan without running it by Mr. Delaney, and that hadn't turned out so well. He wouldn't make that mistake again. He didn't think his plan was far off, but he couldn't risk the money, time, or resources if it was.

He also knew there was a story and lesson behind Ben's parting comment at the café about a man with an ax.

To a man with an ax, everything looks like a tree.

Phillip hadn't chopped anything since their last meeting, so he was probably safe. At least he thought so.

Phillip's call was greeted with the standard, "Ben Delaney. How may I help you?" Phillip did it again, smiled at the greeting, and was certain he'd smile every time he heard Ben answer the phone in the future, too. It was just Ben being Ben.

"Hello, my friend. It's Phil. How are you?" Yes, Phillip actually called *himself* Phil. He hadn't called himself Phil since his dad passed away, and he'd felt like he needed to grow up faster to help his mother.

"You'll rarely find me doing less than fantastic, Phil. Today is no exception. So how goes sales transformation?" Ben figured he wouldn't be hearing from Phillip if things were going exactly like the new CSO wanted.

"Great actually," Phillip answered with genuine enthusiasm. "I finally feel like we're making progress.

"Our conversation about motivation and ownership really, really hit home. My mistakes were painfully obvious, but I believe we're on a better path. The good news is no one, the board included, thought transformation would happen overnight. Everyone realizes it's a long-term investment and knows the return will be well worth the effort."

"Good, Phil. I couldn't be happier to hear it. And how are you coming on the five questions?" Ben reached over to his humidor to look through his stock of timers.

"Would you be surprised if I told you I was still working on the second question?" Phillip didn't mind if Ben were surprised, but he didn't want the older man to be disappointed.

"As far as I know, Phil, sales transformation isn't a timed event. In my opinion, it's more important to do what's right than to do what's fast."

Wow. How many times did I hear my dad say those exact words?

Ben stuck a cigar in his shirt pocket and continued the conversation. "So which part are you stumped by? Are you struggling with the universal truth, or are you struggling with your process providing value to your customers?"

"It's actually a bit of both, Ben. They're obviously closely tied." Phillip said. Before getting to the meat of his answer he took a deep breath, loud enough for Ben to hear clearly at the other end of the line. "I know we have to have much more customer involvement in our sales process so we can bring them greater value. When we looked closely at the process we've developed, we found it was focused on what our salespeople needed to win, not what our customers needed to make the best decision and receive greater value. So I put together a team of our top salespeople, some folks from our learning organization, and a group from product marketing to brainstorm."

If they had been at the café instead of on the telephone, Phillip would have noticed the look on Ben's face and realized his newly found mentor knew where things were headed. Without Ben's face in front of him, Phillip continued presenting his new idea with enthusiasm.

"So we put the buyer's perspective first and developed a program that demonstrates the value of our products and services from their point of view instead of ours. Cool, huh?" Phillip asked without waiting for an answer. "We've been guessing about what's most valuable to our customers. This program is going to get our customers actively involved in determining what would have the greatest impact and most significant value for them. It also broadens their exposure to our full portfolio."

When Phillip stopped talking, the silence was deafening. The pause without comment seemed interminable, with each second feeling like a minute. If it had gone on much longer, Phillip might have even begun to sweat, but Ben finally broke the silence.

"Well, my friend, as I said when I last saw you, to a man with ax, everything looks like a tree. I have a Churchill in my shirt pocket and an open schedule for the next couple of hours. Shall we meet at our café?"

"Aw, Ben, I swear I thought the ax comment was about not firing people or cutting programs, and I haven't done either. I really thought I was safe. I guess I was wrong. Again." Phillip started packing his notepad and pen with his free hand. "I can be there in twenty minutes."

Phillip thought of his father as he was preparing to leave. Getting up to grab his briefcase to meet Ben at the café felt almost like getting up to grab a ball and glove to ride his bike to the ball field and meet his dad. If his father called right as he was leaving work, the time it took him to drive to the field would perfectly match the time it would take Phillip to reach it by bike. Phillip remembered how he felt waiting for his dad to call. He was every bit as anxious, it seemed, to meet again with Ben.

Just as it was the last time, Ben was already seated outside at the café when Phillip arrived. As Phillip approached the table, he was a bit surprised that Ben stood and reached out to him with both arms.

"Time you learned I'm a hugger, Phil. We know each other well enough to drop the handshake. If you're uncomfortable, well, then you'll just have to get over it because if you want to hang out with me, and maybe get a little help, hugs are part of the deal."

Phillip was surprised that he felt no discomfort at all, even though it was only the fourth time he had seen this man. He opened his arms and gave Ben a big hug and three hardy pats on the back.

"Not a problem with me, Ben," he said. "Hugs are a small price to pay for what I'm learning from you, and a whole lot cheaper than me having to pay for your cigars and tea."

Phillip opened his case and grabbed a mockup of a single-sheet brochure as he pressed the power button on his laptop. "I have some things to show you, Ben. I see you haven't fired up the timer, so while you do, I'll get set up. I'm not going to bore you with a long, drawn-out presentation, but I want to give you a sense of my direction."

As Phillip's computer booted, Ben set his cigar off to the side and picked up Phillip's mock brochure. As Phillip typed his username and passcode, Ben held his hand up and said, "Is what you're about to show me on your computer pretty much the same thing I'm looking at here?"

"Uh, yeah, Ben, pretty much. Is that a problem?" Phillip's hands were poised over the keyboard, ready to open his presentation program, but the little finger on his right hand just hovered over one key. Suddenly Phillip was hesitant to press "enter." That was about all the delay needed, because Ben reached over and gently pushed the screen down and closed the laptop.

"I hope closing the lid didn't corrupt your presentation file," he said, "but by the time we're through talking today, you probably won't care."

"Well, if I don't need my laptop, I take it I need my notepad, right?" Phillip reached into the outer pocket of his briefcase and pulled out his pad of paper. Ben saw that Phillip had kept the notes from the last meeting intact. He also noticed that Phillip has added comments from their meeting in Bill Travis's backyard. *Cool.*

"It's great you're keeping all of this in one place, but I'd prefer you transcribe your notes to a computer document. It's not only important stuff for you now, but you may want to do something with it one day," Ben said in a way that was, by intention, fatherly.

"Got it, Ben. I know it needs to get done. Plus, using all this paper means a lot of axes chopping a lot of trees. Which reminds me…" Phillip made a little show of picking up his pen as if his last statement was a question.

"Great transition, my friend," Ben said with an appreciative smile.

Phillip watched intently as Ben went through the process of properly lighting his tobacco timer. He knew once it was done, Ben's next lesson on sales transformation would begin.

"Well, Phil, you've already figured out that the African proverb about a man with an ax has nothing to do with chopping anything. Actually, the quote was intended to help you avoid exactly what you have created here on this brochure," Ben said, picking up the brochure and then pointing it toward Phillip's laptop to finish with, "and, more than likely, in your computer presentation."

Phillip rested his pen on his notepad. "Okay, now I'm confused. How so?"

"In this case, a more appropriate interpretation of the proverb might be 'If you've got an ax in your hand, all you *notice* is trees.'" Ben reached down for his Churchill and contributed a couple more small clouds to the beautiful blue sky they were sitting under. He wanted to pause long enough for the proverb's new version to sink in.

"You see, Phil, all of the products, features, and functions listed on this brochure are nothing more than axes. When your salespeople approach a customer with technology, they look for places where the technology can be applied, just like a man with an ax would look for trees to chop." Ben used his cigar to point to the trees across the street at the ball field. "Don't get me wrong. Taking an ax to a customer would be fine if their problem is trees that need chopping. If the problem is anything else, approaching them with an ax may not be the best strategy."

Phillip didn't even try to hide his grin. "Man, was I way off the mark with that proverb, or what?"

"Just a wee bit," Ben said as he picked up the brochure again. "There is a possibility, if you take this route, your salespeople will get lucky, knock on someone's door with their ax to sell, and have the customer say 'Fantastic! It's the ax man.' Unfortunately, it just won't happen enough. It will be the exception, not the rule."

"So what is the answer, Ben? We've got to show our customers that we have unique capabilities, and we really thought this would be a way to get our customers involved in an open conversation about technology, to let them tell us what was valuable to them. If this isn't a good way to find out, then what is?"

It almost sounded as if Phillip wasn't defending himself, but his entire team.

"The question is, do you want to be a just another technology vendor, or a trusted partner and advisor for your customers?" Once again Ben went on to answer his own question. "After all our conversations about sales transformation, I would highly suspect it's the latter, right?"

"Correct," Phillip replied.

"Then you have to change the conversation you have with your customers altogether." Ben picked up his Churchill and took a long and deliberate draw. As a familiar white puff of smoke left his mouth, he looked down at Phillip's blank sheet on the notepad and said, "Time to start taking notes, Phil."

The younger man did as suggested.

"I've seen it happen time and time again. A lot of organizations spend countless man-hours and dollars making certain everyone on their sales team fully understands their company's product and service offerings. It's amazing the lengths they will go to. Have you considered going the 'product specialists' route yet, Phil?"

"Geez, you make me crazy sometimes, Ben. I swear it feels like you are watching me. Building a product specialist team was one of the ideas from our brainstorming session. Now you've got me waiting for your other flip flop to drop. Is that a good thing or a bad thing?" Phillip was hoping for good.

"I haven't been spying, Phil. You have to get over that. The feeling of me watching you just means you're not alone," Ben said with an encouraging tone. "Product specialists with a ton of knowledge on certain technologies, feature-sets, and functions have become the norm for lots of organizations trying to find ways to differentiate their approach and bring additional value to their customers."

Ben held the brochure up again.

"When you ask these specialists a question, they can quote chapter and verse from product and service manuals inches thick. I'm not joking. It's freakish to watch. Unfortunately, we are molding these folks to be better technologists, not better business people. And that's a huge, huge problem if you're trying to transform your sales organization."

"Yeah, but doesn't their depth of knowledge provide some value to the customers?" Phillip asked. He let out a groan that sounded as if he were pleading to be right this time.

"Of course it can sometimes, but you have to remember your specialists are focused on their axes, not the customers' problems. If your customer has a tree to chop, you're golden, otherwise..." Ben let the rest go unsaid, then continued on. "Look, for your company to reach the status of trusted advisor, you're going to have to be seen as a long-term partner, someone whose contributions are part of your customer's ongoing success. An ax isn't gonna solve all their problems. If you're going to be a key contributor to your customer, you have to shift the conversation from your ax—the technology, features, and functions on this brochure—to the customer's business. You have to be better business people.

"Let me ask you a question, Phil. Who in your customers' businesses do your people typically meet with? What departments do they interact with?"

Phillip knew Ben wasn't going to like his answer. "They meet with people in the information technology department. The IT folks are typically responsible for buying and managing all the things we sell."

Phillip was right. Ben didn't like his answer. But he didn't dislike it either. It was the truth, which was all Ben wanted.

"So you're basically taking your ax to only those people in your customer's organization who are responsible for managing trees. What the heck else will they talk about but chopping? If you want to be a true business advisor and partner, Phil, you have to put away your ax and move away from the forest. Your contacts have to shift from the IT and purchasing departments to people throughout your customer's whole organization."

Phillip took his pen away from the paper, stopped taking notes, and leaned back in his chair to absorb yet another revelation about sales from the man he'd beaten out for his current CSO position. Ben noticed the shift in position, so he reached over to his cigar, picked it up, took a moment to admire its beauty and the way it felt in his fingertips, then proceeded to enjoy the act of drawing it back to life with a couple of quick puffs. When Phillip looked like he'd had enough time and was ready to move onto the next thought, Ben put the cigar back down gently and, not quite so gently, continued the lesson.

"Okay, so now you've got this brochure and presentation with fifty different things on it, asking customers if any of it's beneficial to them. C'mon, Phil, don't you see how funny that is?" Ben asked as he dismissed Phillip's newest idea. "It's like you're a solution in search of a problem. So you can train all your specialists to be walking, talking product manuals, but if they don't know enough about their customers' issues outside the IT department to demonstrate measurable impact on what the customer is trying to accomplish with their business, it won't matter. It's a complete waste of everyone's time.

"And that, my friend, is a crime." Ben shook his head in disgust at the thought as he picked up his cigar to gauge the time they had left.

Phil eagerly picked up his pen again. "So what should they know, Ben? If not our axes, what specific things should we be focused on?"

"Think about being a good business partner, Phil. Would a good partner fully understand the business's vision? Would a good partner know what *business* goals are in place to support that vision? Would they know what plans were in place to meet those goals? Would they thoroughly understand *business* processes? Would they know the company's strengths, weaknesses, opportunities, and threats?"

Phillip couldn't take notes much faster, but he was nodding and tossing an occasional "uh-huh" into the conversation. He was way too busy to look up. Ben leaned forward with his hand rested on the table just a couple of inches away from Phillip. He wanted to make sure the next point wasn't missed.

"If you guys want to be unique, to truly differentiate your products, services, and approach, you've got to get off the technology wagon," Ben said, adding sternly, "Never lead with this brochure or anything like it.

"You have to realize what will make your people stand apart from the crowd. The *only* true differentiator of your products and services will be the amount of measurable impact you have on what your customers are trying to accomplish as a business. If you don't know their vision and goals, their plans and processes, you can't demonstrate how you impact those areas in some meaningful, measurable way. Heck, Phil, then you end up being just another vendor peddling the same basic things as your competitors."

Phillip took the brochure from Ben's hand, balled it up, and then was met with more stern, fatherly-like advice after his unsuccessful three-point attempt at the trashcan by the café door.

"You may want to pick that up, Phil. It's trash to you, but competitive intelligence to others." Phillip hopped up, slightly embarrassed but enjoying the moment of hustling like a kid to grab the rebound of his errant shot. The makeshift basketball didn't get dunked like his instinct told him to. Phillip decided to hold the ball until time ran out. In the few seconds it took to return to the table, Ben had put away his cigar clipper and lighter. There was a little cigar left, but the story was surely coming to a close.

"You know, Phil, it doesn't even matter what's on that list of technology you're holding. There are others who do a lot of those same things. When you go into your customer's business to meet with the same IT people as your competitors, and then you talk about the same technology as your competitors, how do you expect them to see you any differently?" Ben readied the story's bottom line: "In those cases, when it comes time for them to buy, price becomes the determining factor."

"Our margins suck." Phillip hadn't said that to anyone outside his organization. He got over the guilt of saying it, and quickly. It was just a matter of the simple truth between friends.

"You want to drive your margins up?" Ben pointed his cigar skyward. "Then you have to change the conversation. Start having business conversations with your customers and understand how they measure success before talking about your products and services. If you want to get the conversation off price, then become the trusted partner. You have to be able to provide significant strategic value by demonstrating measurable impact on things like your customer's productivity and efficiency, image, expenses, revenue, safety, security, and stability. Your people have to be able to justify a higher price by proving greater impact and return. Period."

"So back to the drawing board?" Phillip asked while rubbing his temples.

"Probably so," Ben replied with his more familiar gentle smile. "The good news is, once you fix this part of your process, you'll probably be able to answer yes to the remainder of the first five questions."

"The first five? You have more?" Phillip lowered his head as if the weight of answering more questions had pulled it down. Still sitting close, Ben reached forward a little and tapped Phillip's notepad with a finger.

"Oh, heck, yeah," he said. "There are more questions for you to answer. If this were easy, you and everybody else would already be transformed by now. Just like the last set, we're looking for you to be able to answer each of these four questions with a yes. When you do, four more obstacles are removed to sales transformation. Okay, you ready?"

"I've got writer's cramp," Phillip said with a smile, as he shook his right hand in the air to stimulate any feeling other than the cramp. "But you keep going. I'll write left-handed if I have to."

Ben held up four fingers.

"Number one, does your formal sales process provide a foundation for your salespeople to understand the customer's business first?

"Number two, are your salespeople talking to a broad spectrum of people in your customer's business outside of IT and/or purchasing?

"And three, can your salespeople tell you the vision, goals, plans, processes, strengths, weaknesses, etc., of their customers outside the realm of your company's products and services? Test this one with some of your reps when you return to your office, Phil. You'll find it interesting."

Phillip wrote the words "test tomorrow" next to that question.

Ben had one finger remaining. "And one last one for you today. Are you or your salespeople regularly invited to your customer's business to discuss their driving business issues as a strategic partner *before* there is an obvious need for what you sell?"

"Is that it?" Phillip asked as he put his pen down and flexed his fingers. "I swear I may never be able to write again."

"Trust me, that's plenty," Ben said as he tapped the side of Phillip's note pad with his finger.

As if on cue, their server opened the café door and started walking toward their table holding the check for iced tea. He would have reached the table unnoticed had he not been humming an unrecognizable tune, horribly out of key. Without looking in the waiter's direction, both Ben and Phillip winced in mock pain.

"Hopefully, this will be over soon," Ben said as he tipped his head in the waiter's direction.

"I may never listen to music again," Phillip added, his eyes squinting with each note.

As the cheery waiter reached the table, Ben said, "Excuse me. I'm curious. What's the name of that song you're humming? I'm challenging my friend here to a game of name-that-tune and this one has us stumped."

"Oh, it's a song by a singer-songwriter named David Mead. You probably wouldn't know him. It's called 'Chatterbox.' Don't feel bad. It would have stumped almost anybody." Thankfully, the question and response momentarily stopped the humming, all part of Ben's plan.

"Anything else for you guys today?" asked the waiter.

"Nope," Phillip answered, adding, "Not unless you have something for a really bad headache that just came on."

Ben almost lost his last mouthful of iced tea as he let out a hardy laugh, while Phillip giggled his way through, "Just kidding. Thanks, though. We're really fine."

The singing server placed the check on the table and, without hesitation or improvement in pitch, walked back toward the café, humming "Chatterbox" a little louder than before.

"There's a lesson for all of us, Phil. Never take singing lessons from someone who is tone deaf," Ben said as put the heels of his hands on his eyes and waited for the café door to shut behind the waiter and the painful sound to stop. As soon as it did, Ben began the ritual of extinguishing his timer.

Phillip seized the opportunity to capitalize on Ben's distraction, looked over the older man's shoulder in mock surprise and said, "Oh, my gosh, would you look at that!"

Ben turned and looked, of course, and didn't see anything out of the ordinary behind him. But when he turned back, the check for the day's ice tea had disappeared from the tabletop.

"Wow. I'm surprised a wise old man like you fell for such an old trick," Phillip said while proudly waving the check as if it was the prize in a game of keep-away.

"C'mon, kiddo, trust me. I stayed turned around until I was certain you picked up the check."

As the two men stood to leave, Phillip remembered Ben was a hugger, so he opened his arms and waited.

Ben obliged with a hug and just before it ended, he told Phillip, "Remember what I said. That's a lesson for all of us. Never take singing lessons from someone who is tone deaf."

"Trust me, Ben," Phillip replied quickly. "I can't sing. No amount of lessons would help."

As Ben released the hug and walked toward his car, he said, "That's not why I said it…"

CHAPTER 7

Don't Take Singing Lessons from a Tone-Deaf Instructor

In the office again, the day after his meeting with Ben Delaney and with his back turned toward his tenth-floor view of the city below, Phillip Hawthorne stared at his computer monitor. The nine sales transformation questions posed by Ben during their last two meetings stared back. Phillip knew that each time one of these questions could be answered with a "yes," he had removed a major obstacle to transforming his sales organization. He also knew there were more questions in store.

Phillip thought about how oddly comfortable his relations with Ben had become. They'd had a contentious beginning, trapped in a small waiting room while the board of directors decided which of them had won the battle of the interviews. At the time, he hoped to never see Ben Delaney again. But by now he was calling the old man, asking for meetings and looking forward to it anytime he knew he was having iced tea at the outdoor café to learn more about sales—and life. Ben, despite Phillip's first impression in that waiting room, was actually fun to hang out with.

Phillip chuckled out loud remembering Ben's reaction to the waiter humming. *Ah…who was it…oh yeah, David Mead. The song was "Chatterbox," right?* If Mr. Mead sounded like the waiter, it was no wonder Phillip hadn't heard the song. No radio station would play it. Who would buy it?

Phillip Hawthorne, that's who. What a great idea. He fired up his browser and typed in "David Mead Chatterbox" and there it was on the album "Tangerine" from Tallulah Media. What a trip! He went to his favorite Internet music service, found the song, and selected "gift to a friend." As the song played from his desktop speakers, Phillip typed a message to send Ben with his present.

> Dear Ben,
>
> I thought you would find this interesting. It's hard to imagine this is the same song our waiter was humming. Mead can actually sing! It's obvious he was aware of THIS axiom: Never take singing lessons from someone who is tone deaf! Thanks again for all your help! Phil

Phillip felt a little guilt over the insignificance of an MP3 file in comparison to all Ben had done for him, but hey, it was the thought that counted. And he was certain when all was said and done, he would find something far grander to give Ben as payment, even though he suspected that the satisfaction of a fully transformed sales organization was all Ben expected in return.

Phillip went back to his list of sales transformation questions and continued the process of determining who in his organization would be responsible for what. He worked all the way down to the sixth question and just as he began to type a note to the head of his learning organization, Phillip's mobile phone began to ring. Phillip saw Ben's number in his caller ID. *Wow, that was quick.*

"Phillip Hawthorne. How may I help you?" Phillip answered.

"Very funny, Phil. I spent the better part of an hour working on three or four different ways to answer my phone, and you do this to me?" Ben sounded completely serious.

"Relax, Ben. I saw your name on my caller ID," Phillip responded with a satisfied smile that Ben could see through the phone line. "Trust me, I would never answer my phone with a greeting you stole from some retail outlet."

"Okay, I'm listening to this song and I refuse to believe it's the same one our waiter was humming. There is no way a song could be butchered that bad. Really, no way," Ben said as Phillip's gifted song played in the background.

"Yep. I know I have more important things to do, but I couldn't resist. The Internet makes it too easy. All of a sudden, finding and buying that song for you became my number-one priority. I couldn't stand the thought of you losing a game of name-that-tune," Phillip said. At that same moment he realized how childish that probably sounded coming from a C-level executive.

"Well, my friend, as long as you realize how important the message was, I'm fine with you making it a priority," Ben replied.

However slightly, Phillip's head jerked back at Ben's statement. "What? What message? Oh, come on Ben. There was a lesson?"

Ben replied slowly, "Phil, when I said it, was my cigar still burning?"

Phillip tried to replay the final moments at the café. "I don't remember, Ben. I thought we were finished when you gave me the questions." Now all Phillip could remember was the sound of the waiter's miserable humming.

"You obviously didn't write down one of the first important lessons I gave you. When there's still life in one of ol' Ben Delaney's cigars, there's still life in his story."

Suddenly, Phillip could clearly remember seeing Ben putting his cigar in the ashtray as the waiter stepped back inside the café. "That's right. And you said, 'There's a lesson for all of us, Phil.' You actually said that twice. Unbelievable," he said, shaking his head in disgust. "Geez, sometimes I'm so dense."

Ben sounded fatherly again. "You're not dense, Phil. You just have a lot on your mind."

"And I'm frustrated, Ben. Every time we get together, you leave me with something thought provoking. That is becoming predictable. Unfortunately, so far, my thoughts have been provoked too late to avoid the problems they were intended to eliminate. That's become predictable, too." Phillip knew Ben admired aggression as a character trait. "So today I'm breaking the cycle. I want to start with the lesson and apply it before I stumble. Fair enough?"

"So I not only need to change my telephone greeting, but the order in which I deliver things that are thought provoking as well. Hold on. Let me take a note." Ben rustled paper loud enough for Phillip to hear.

"Okay, who's the funny man now, Ben? Anyway, was the comment about vocal lessons significant enough to warrant a cigar and a meeting at the café?" Phillip suspected it was.

"How about tomorrow at three o'clock?" Ben asked without needing to check his calendar.

"Tomorrow at three p.m. works great for me. See you then." Phillip hung up the phone and immediately started humming a rendition of "Chatterbox" that was far closer to the waiter's than David Mead's.

The next day, Phillip left for the café a full hour and a half earlier than usual. Since predictability had become an entertaining issue with him and Ben, he wanted to show up early enough to be certain he and two glasses of iced tea were already there when Ben arrived. Years ago, an uncle had mentioned that Phillip's dad liked cigars called Montecristos, so he stopped at a tobacco shop on the way and picked up a half dozen of them. He had no idea how much longer or how many more times Ben would be willing to meet with him like this. But it had become more than learning about the company's sales transformation to Phillip, and he was hoping Ben might feel a bit more obligated if he provided the timers for him.

"Yep!" Phillip said to no one in particular. "Right on time." As Phillip suspected he would, Ben pulled into the café parking lot at 2:45, fifteen minutes earlier than their appointed time.

"Oh, come on. Did I have the time wrong, Phil?" Ben asked as he approached the table, pointing to his watch. "How long have you been waiting?"

"I'll never tell, Ben. You have the time right, but if I tell you how long I've been here, next time you'll make sure you're here early enough to beat me, and that ain't happening. You know how competitive I am. I have to be better than you at something." Phillip's big smile at his victory got even bigger when he reached into his bag and pulled out a Montecristo. "I even brought my own clock. Does this work for you?"

Ben picked up the cigar and ran it under his nose. "Ah, talk about memories. This was one of the first cigars I ever smoked. As a matter of fact, it's the same one my dear friend smoked to demonstrate using a cigar as a timer. You have no idea how perfect it is."

"Well, you have no idea how happy that makes me, Ben. That cigar was my dad's favorite." As soon as the words came out of his mouth, Phillip felt a weird combination of excitement and sadness.

Ben pulled out his cutter and lined it up on the base of the Montecristo. "Your dad had good taste, son."

"Well, we lucked out. Our singing server isn't here today. I've asked for his schedule so we can plan our meetings on his days off," Phillip said as seriously as he could.

"Probably getting praise for his rendition of 'Chatterbox' from some tone-deaf instructor," Ben said as he casually flicked his lighter and positioned its flame at the end of the cigar. He and Phillip were able to remain quiet and hold their faces expressionless for almost ten seconds. Phillip was the first to break into laughter with Ben a split-second behind.

The two laughed at the joke for longer than they probably should have. When they settled down and it was time for business, Phillip opened his laptop and turned it on. "That's a great segue, Ben. I feel like I'm a pretty smart guy, but for the life of me, I can't make the leap from singing lessons to sales transformation. It's almost as difficult as the connection to tartar sauce."

"It's just one more universal truth, my friend," Ben said as he lifted his iced tea in a toast to truth.

Phillip raised his glass and proclaimed, "To truth!"

"There are many things you don't know about me, Phillip. I won't bore you with gory details, but growing up I was torn between my mother's dream of me becoming a major league ballplayer and mine of being a rock star. When it came right down to it, I believed my chances with girls were far greater going the rock star route," Ben said while raising his left hand and extending his pinky and index finger in the classic rock-on salute. "I mean look at Keith Richards' mug, and he's dated some of the most gorgeous women in the world!"

Phillip grinned and shook his head. "I know. It's unbelievable."

"So I decided 'Why not me?' I learned to play drums, dropped out of college, and spent two years traveling with a band. Becoming a rock star? I got the rock part, 'cause that life couldn't have been any harder. The star half never quite happened. I eventually figured I could either continue playing or eat, and I chose food. My adoring female fans had to wait. I quit the band after playing one last gig on a wild spring-break weekend in Ft. Lauderdale." Ben drew on his cigar and blew a couple of perfect smoke rings.

"Anyway, the music bug has never quite gotten out of my system. I don't think it ever will. You think I'm too old to do it now, Phil?" Ben asked in a way that seemed only half-joking to Phil.

"You're never too old to rock and roll, Ben. Think about it. Even though he's looked like death for decades, Keith Richards is still rockin', my man," Phillip replied while returning Ben's rock-on sign with both hands.

"So part of my music curse has become a fascination with these TV singing competitions. I watch every episode of all of them. If I've got something else going on, I've got my DVR set to capture them all. It's an obsession," Ben said almost sheepishly. "If you ever tell anybody, I will hunt you down."

"Don't worry, Ben. For a fee, your secret's safe with me," Phillip said holding his right hand up and rubbing his fingers together.

"Very kind of you, Phil. So anyway, on each of the shows, there is always at least one judge who shows no mercy with the contestants. They hold nothing back. They're typically a Brit with a quick wit and no compassion when it comes to their critiques.

"The first few weeks of the shows are always the early auditions where they show all of the goofballs that get cut. It's hilarious. Some of the people are obviously just looking for their fifteen minutes of fame.

"I remember one flake from last year whose audition made our waiter sound like Sinatra. It was more like a shrieking howl than singing. Thirty seconds into his performance the judges stopped him and the British guy asked, 'Who told you that you can sing?' The contestant's reply? 'My vocal coach, for one.'" Ben smiled recalling the scene on TV again. "And that's where I heard the line.

"This should be a lesson to us all. Never take singing lessons from someone who is tone deaf." Ben picked up his cigar and took three "oh-so-Ben" quick puffs, then looked away.

Phillip waited patiently in silence for several seconds as Ben held his cigar in the corner of his mouth and stared at the Little League ball field. Just as he was about to say something to get the conversation back on track, Ben continued. "At that moment, I thought about sales training."

Phillip sat straight up and shook his head quickly, in disbelief. "You thought about what? Of all things, why in the heck would you think about sales training?"

"Well, actually, the other day here at the café, when the waiter came out humming that awful thing, I thought of the show, the judge, the quote, sales training, then sales transformation, in that order. You want to know why?"

Phillip didn't know whether to type what he was about to hear, or just sit and let it sink in. Phillip was amused. *This is going to be a stretch.*

Actually, it was no stretch at all.

"Here's the simple truth. An instructor who is tone deaf wouldn't be able to tell whether or not a student is singing in key. Having never sung on pitch themselves, how would they know? So I could see a tone-deaf vocal coach telling a student to pick any song they wanted, then applauding the student's first attempt to sing it as if it were a masterful performance. They wouldn't be able to tell the difference." Ben looked at his smoking timer and decided it needed a rest.

"Okay, that's easy. I got it," Phillip said while moving the ashtray and cigar just out of Ben's reach. "You'll get that back when you connect the dots all the way to sales transformation."

"It's really quite simple, Phil. We've been talking about this during our last few times together. When you talk about training as part of sales transformation, it becomes way, way more than the traditional transfer of skills and knowledge. When you take on the task of changing the behaviors of salespeople, we're talking about changing the DNA, the very culture of the organization. That is a MUCH bigger task and obstacle for transformation." Ben started to reach for the ashtray and cigar.

Phillip picked it up and set it on the ground by his feet. "Not so fast, Mr. Ben. You're not quite there yet."

"You can't see the connection, Phil?" Ben held both hands out to his sides, palms up, and shrugged. "Come on, man. Training is the launching pad for your entire sales transformation program. It's huge. You can design a process that you know is right on, but if you can't deliver it properly, it'll fall flat on its face and take you down with it. You gotta make sure the sellers and managers really get it if you want them to change how they act. They have to see how it works in the real world, their world, in front of their customers. Everything falls apart if they don't."

Phillip held his hands out and shrugged to mimic Ben. "So what are you suggesting I do? Test my trainers for perfect pitch?"

"Kinda," Ben said matter-of-factly. "Here it is, Phil. You've been talking about your learning organization since our second meeting. Are these the folks who are going to deliver sales training to your organization?"

"Of course," Phillip said. "That's their responsibility. It's what they're paid to do."

Ben leaned forward and rested his forearm on the table. "Do you know if any of these trainers were ever successful salespeople?"

Another revelation flooded Phillip's head. He thought about the trainers on the staff of his learning organization. They were all great people, but he was certain none of them had ever been successful sellers. If they had been, that would probably be what they were still doing.

Phillip decided to test his revelation with Ben. "So what you are saying is that if my trainers don't have selling experience, they wouldn't know whether a student's performance was off key or not."

"Can I have my cigar back?" Ben asked, holding his hand out. Phillip obliged.

"Not exactly, my friend. While it might be a plus if they have sold before, it's not their experience that concerns me; it's their credibility." Ben picked up his cigar and puffed life back into it.

"Delivering technical training is very different than delivering sales training. You're not gonna get a ton of push-back when you're teaching features and functions. The material is what it is. Sales methodology and process is a whole lot different. Most of these folks come to class thinking they already know how to sell. Now they got some hotshot instructor who's never sold before telling them how to do their job? Whoa.

"So what I'm saying is you can't just put anybody in front of your sales team. They have to be screened and tested. They can't be tone deaf. They have to be able to sing. You know what I mean?" Bill didn't wait for Phillip to answer. "You have to be sure they can demonstrate new skills in a compelling and believable fashion. If they can't, your sellers won't be able to see how these new skills apply to their reality. And it can't be just people in your learning organization that are the final judges of whether or not your instructors are credible. It's got to be their internal customers, your salespeople, the folks they're going to train."

Phil leaned back in his chair as if basking in the glow of Ben's wisdom. "I have to admit I didn't think you would be able to make the connection, Ben, but you are right on again. Remarkable."

"Why thank you, Phil. It took a while, but I finally got us where I wanted to go." Satisfied that Phillip had accepted another sales transformation lesson, Ben sat back in his chair, picked up his cigar, and propped his feet on the chair next to him.

"While we're still on the subject of sales training, there's something else you should know." Ben lifted his right hand and vigorously scratched the back of his head as if he were stirring up brain cells.

"The floor is still yours, Mr. Delaney. I'm all ears and fingers." Phillip put his hands back on his keyboard.

"I'm gonna stay on the music theme for a moment, if I may." Ben picked up a placemat and held it up to Phillip. "Let's say this is sheet music. Do you know how a singer learns a new song, Phil?"

"By practicing?" Phil answered tentatively.

"It's not just by practicing. It's how they practice. They learn it a line at a time, my friend. They get the lyrics and melody for one line before they move to the next. Once they're done with all the lines, they put them all together to make the song." Ben looked at Phillip to see if this connection to sales transformation was going to happen quicker than the others.

"I think I get it, Ben." Phillip stopped talking and looked at Ben. "We've got to teach the process a line at a time. Once they've learned all the lines, or in other words, the entire program a piece at a time, they can put it all together at the end."

"That's part of it, Phil. In your program, it's all about the facilitation of incremental change. Sales transformation doesn't mean everything changes at once. Changing everything now is not just improbable; it's impossible. The process has to be broken down into bite-sized pieces, each foundational, each standing on its own logic and truth. Sales transformation happens by changing one behavior at a time over time. You can't expect to put your folks in a classroom and have them leave transformed. It's a work in progress, Phil. The program has to be designed to help every individual master each piece of the process, one line at a time, until your folks change all the behavior you and they want to change."

Ben looked at his watch and frowned. "Well, my friend, it's time to pack up. I'm headed to get a quick haircut then have a beer with my old friend Tom Keenan. The poor guy's a homebuilder. That's certainly not a business I would want to be in right now. You'd love him, though. He's a techno-geek just like you. He'll have his laptop in the pub. He calls it a tool of the trade. I call it a huge, expensive metal coaster." Ben shook his head as he stared down at the last of his cigar. "I remember when a homebuilder's 'tools of the trade' were hammers, nails, saws, and levels."

Phillip smiled and said with mock empathy, "Oh, poor Ben. Are you missing the good old days?"

Ben gently extinguished his cigar as he spoke. "No, my friend. The days are always as good as you make them. To me, the new ones are as good as the old. Sometimes I just think a homebuilder with a laptop has lost connection with the people and tools that actually build the house. I'm sure Tom's business card still says 'Homebuilder,' but he hasn't really built anything in years." Ben looked at his watch. "Shoot, I really gotta get going.

"While your computer is still on, I want to give you some more questions to add to your sales transformation list. You want to add to it?"

Phil stretched his fingers, cracked his knuckles, and prepared to type. "I wouldn't let you leave without giving them to me."

"I'm not going to wear your fingers out today, Phil. There are just three questions. They're all important, and we're still looking for a yes on each one."

In traditional Ben delivery style, he lifted three fingers.

"One. Have you tested your trainers to make certain they have the skills necessary to train salespeople?

"Two. Does your instructor training include them proving they can demonstrate new sales skills in a compelling and believable fashion to their internal customer, your salespeople?"

"And three. Are your formal sales process and training delivery designed to facilitate incremental improvement over time? In other words, are they developed to improve one skill at a time over time?"

Phillip finished typing the last question, let out a big sigh, and sat back in his chair. "This stuff makes so much sense, Ben. Have you ever thought of writing all this down?"

Ben smiled. "Why would I write it down when you are doing such an excellent job of typing it for me?"

"So true, Ben." Phillip thought of closing his laptop but decided to leave it open and, once again, stay a step ahead of his mentor. There was little doubt Ben had another cliffhanger coming as he walked to his car. The intro to the next lesson was only seconds away.

Ben got up from the table and stumbled a little to his left. "Dang it, Phil. An old man like me can't sit with his legs this way for long without at least one of his feet going to sleep." He shook his right foot and stomped it on the patio tile.

Okay, here it comes. It will be something about sleeping feet. What could feet falling asleep have to do with sales transformation?

"Iced tea is paid for, Ben, so there'll be no race for the check," Phillip said as he typed a note about Ben's feet falling asleep.

"Well, thank you again for everything, my friend," Ben said as he gave Phillip what looked like a cross between a salute and a tip of the hat. "Call if you need me!"

Ben stared over at the Little League field as he walked toward his car. Phillip waited patiently for the continuation of a story about feet falling asleep. It never came.

"Is that it?" Phillip said to the empty patio as Ben shut his door and started his car. He realized his hands were still over his keyboard as Ben's car left the parking lot and drove slowly past the ball field. "Sleeping feet? Really?"

CHAPTER 8

Never Use a Screwdriver to Hammer a Nail

Phillip's sales transformation spreadsheet had now grown by three more questions, twelve questions total. His patience, though, had not grown at all. Phillip knew he was still looking at an incomplete roadmap, an unfinished schematic. While Ben had been extremely generous with his time, Phillip wanted more. He sat at his desk and wondered how he could make that happen without being overbearing. Phillip didn't want to push Ben too far. He was, after all, working for free.

Wait a minute. Does Ben have to work for free? Why couldn't I just hire him as a consultant? He was still retired and hadn't yet totally devoted himself to Chairman Bill's tartar sauce business. Phillip had certainly gotten significant value from every meeting with Ben. So far, all it had cost was iced tea and a Montecristo cigar, neither of which Phillip expensed to the company. He wondered whether or not Ben would even consider it. The more he thought about it, the more he thought Ben would. As a matter of fact, Phillip couldn't imagine any reason Ben wouldn't. There was only one way to find out.

Phillip reached for his telephone.

"Ben Delaney. What's up?" Ben answered with what was, obviously, a new telephone greeting.

"I liked your other greeting way better, Ben." Phillip really meant it. The old greeting was more "Ben", especially the "How may I help you?" part.

"Okay, then," Ben said quickly. "Ben Delaney. What's up? How may I help you? Is that better?"

"Better," Phillip said. "But one of the ways to make the new days as good as the old days would be if you went back to your old greeting, Ben. I'm not proud you changed it on account of me."

"I've got a secret for you. You're the only one who will hear that particular greeting. You're not the only person with caller ID, you know. The Ben Delaney retail outlet greeting still lives and breathes for everyone but you, Phil."

"Gee, thanks," Phillip said. "I'm blocking my number when I call you from this point forward. I want the same old greeting everyone else gets."

"Do what you need to do, Phil," Ben said. "I did my best for you. Anyway, since it's your favorite, I'll say this part again…How may I help you?"

"You have already helped me, Ben, in immeasurable ways. And you've been so generous with your time. But for me, it's just not enough. At least it's not happening fast enough." Phillip suddenly realized how selfish and childish he might sound. "I don't want to appear spoiled, Ben, but I want to get a clearer view of everything ahead of me."

"So what are you saying? Do you want me to raise my one cigar, one story maximum?" Ben smiled at the thought of how much his and Phillip's relationship had changed.

"No, Ben. As a matter of fact, I don't want to be restricted by a cigar timer any more, and I want you to be fairly compensated for your time and effort. What would you say if I offered you a stint as a paid consultant?"

"You want the short answer, Phil?" Ben said abruptly.

Phillip was surprised at Ben's tone. "I don't know that I've ever gotten a short answer from you, Ben, but sure."

"No."

It wasn't that Phillip hadn't been prepared for the possibility of Ben turning down the offer. He was just surprised at how quickly and absolutely it came. He tried to collect his thoughts but couldn't, then said, "Wow. That was quick. Maybe I should have asked for the long answer."

"Well, you should know me well enough to figure out I would follow with the long answer." Ben's tone was, well, back to Ben. "It's not that I haven't enjoyed working with you, Phil. It's been a pleasure, a dream actually. I just could never charge you for what I am doing. Hopefully you will understand some day."

"I *don't* understand, Ben. You have something of value to my company and me. I believe any investment we make in your services will provide a good return. If you've got the time, I've got money in my sales transformation budget. The board and the CEO already know and like you, and my ego can accept that I could use your help. Are you telling me you're so flush with retirement cash you couldn't use the extra money?"

"It's not the money, Phil. You know I have an expensive cigar habit, so I could use every dollar. I just can't accept money for what I am giving you, and if you can't accept that, we may have a problem. I don't want to stop helping you, but I will if you insist. And I sincerely mean that." Ben hoped Phillip sensed the finality of his statement.

"Okay, Ben. I accept it, but I don't think I will ever understand it." Phillip's disappointment was clear in the delivery of his response.

"Now you've put me in a difficult position. I want to accelerate this process. I love your cliffhangers, but I can't wait for the punch line like I have been. So how do we do make this happen faster without me giving you some incentive?"

"I've received all the incentive I need, Phil," Ben said. "All you've had to do this far is ask for help. Have I ever refused you?"

"No, Ben. I just worry there'll come a time you will, and I've got too much on the line here." Phillip caught himself again. The more he spoke, the more selfish he believed he sounded. "My people and my company have too much on the line, Ben. It's not just me. Our entire organization needs your help."

"Then my help you will have, my friend." Ben sounded fatherly again. "Chairman Bill is busy being chairman of the County Commission right now anyway, so just tell me what you need."

"Just more time, Ben," Phillip replied. "Just more time."

"Okay, here's the deal, Phil. I'll always have a one-cigar/one-story maximum, and that's a good thing for you. Each and every story I tell has to stand on its own. Trust me. You don't want me mixing stories or stacking them up on you, either. Both our heads would explode into a gooey mess if I did." Ben chuckled at how funny that sounded, but how truthful it probably was.

"Well how much more is there, Ben?" Phillip wondered if this meant another meeting or another ten.

"There are twenty-five questions that require a yes answer. By my count, you and I are at number twelve. How many Montecristos did you buy?"

"As many as you can smoke, Ben. As a matter of fact, I've got five in my bag and already have the beginning of the story about your foot falling asleep in a document on my computer. I typed it as you were leaving the café." Phillip was as smug as he had ever been. "And I even have some ideas about where the story is going."

"What story?" Ben sounded sincerely perplexed. "Was I telling a story?"

"Oh, come on, Ben. The last thing you say before we part is always the beginning of your next story." Phillip was certain Ben was pulling his leg. "Don't mess with me, Delaney. You said you couldn't sit with your feet on the chair that long. You stomped your foot to wake it up. Remember?"

"I have a question for you, Hawthorne." Ben was cool with the fact they were suddenly on a last-name basis. "Was my cigar still burning when I told you my foot was asleep?"

Oh no. Why does this always happen? Phillip, once again, found himself mentally recounting the last minutes at the café. And again, he recalled Ben snuffing out his cigar *before* he got up from the table.

"You're right, Ben. Your cigar was out when you stood up." All Phillip could do was stare out his tenth-floor window and shake his head. "Why can't I get this?"

"Beats me, Phil. You're the young one." Ben knew how much that statement must have bothered the younger and very competitive Phillip Evan Hawthorne. "I established the Ben Delaney rules of storytelling at Bill's fish fry, and I've reminded you each time we've met since. What more could I do?"

"Meet with me every day until I have all twenty-five questions, for one," Phillip demanded. "Two, you can tell me if there was something I missed from our last meeting. If it wasn't your foot falling asleep, what was it?"

"Are you telling me you aren't the sharpest *tool* in the shed, Phillip? Do I have to *hammer* this in to you? You couldn't *nail* it on your own?" Ben paused in amusement at his vocal emphasis.

"No, I'm obviously not the sharpest *tool* in the shed. I'm surprised you didn't try to *level* with me." As he spoke, Phillip began to type a message to his administrative assistant cancelling anything on his afternoon calendar for the next several days. "You're killing me. Can't you just go have a beer with an old friend without tying it to a story?"

"Why would I?" Though Ben paused, it was obvious he wasn't posing a rhetorical question. "Can you meet me at our spot in an hour?"

"I couldn't imagine being anywhere else. See you then," Phillip said as he began packing his laptop and the remaining five Montecristos.

Phillip left the office immediately. This time, though, it had nothing to do with engaging Ben in a competitive battle for first arrival. He wanted every minute he could in Ben's company. If Ben was going to arrive 15 minutes early, Phillip wanted all 15 of those minutes.

Phillip arrived at the café half an hour early. He ordered two large iced teas, then placed a Montecristo, a newly purchased cigar lighter, and a cutter on the placemat in front of Ben's chair. Once again, this wasn't just a courtesy to Ben. It was an effort to maximize every moment they had together. He probably picked up two extra minutes with this little preparation.

Ben provided an additional bonus by pulling in to the café parking lot twenty minutes early. Just as Phillip had done, Ben left for the café minutes after their conversation ended. He was as excited to get to work as Phillip was.

As Ben approached the table, he held his arms out for a hug. As Phillip stood to greet him, he realized the hug was no longer just for Ben. It was a way for Phillip to show him the sincerity of his gratitude and the level of respect Ben had earned. As Ben began to release the hug, Phillip held on for second or two longer. He hadn't felt that same emotion since he was a twelve-year-old boy hugging his dad when they met at the ball field.

Ben looked over Phillip's shoulder to the tabletop. "Let's see...a Montecristo, cutter, lighter, and ashtray. I take it the iced tea is on the way?"

"That is correct, sir," Phillip responded as a private would to a captain.

"So I have all the tools I need for today's meeting. You've got your laptop and a curious mind, so you've got all the tools you need. Good." Ben picked up the cutter and cigar and began to prepare his work surface. A non-singing server delivered the iced tea, and a flick of the lighter signaled the beginning of the next lesson on sales transformation.

"Man, I had a great time at the pub with my friend Tom. I've been talking tartar sauce with Bill and technology with you, so it was good to switch gears a bit and talk about something different. No offense to either you or Bill. Sometimes it's good to translate your ideas for other types of businesses. It allows me to test for contradictions to what I believe to be universal truths." Ben sat back in his chair and admired his Monetcristo.

"Did you find any contradictions?" Phillip suspected the answer was no, and from Ben's grin he knew that's the answer he would get.

"Not a one." Ben's grin turned in to a wide smile. "Sometimes I'm amazed at how circumstances fall into place. It just so happens my conversation with Tom is directly tied to our next sales transformation topic."

"How so?" Phillip used the tool of his curious mind.

"Tom is struggling as a homebuilder. Sales are slow, margins are slim, and he has been desperate to find ways to do more with less. He bought a new laptop and dumped a ton of money into management software to help him become more productive and efficient. He's seen a difference in his daily routine, but isn't certain anything he is doing is having any impact on what he wants his final product to be—a well-built home.

"So I asked Tom how his *workers* used his laptop and the management software." Ben paused to shave ash off his cigar and give Phillip's curious mind a moment to consider where this story may be going.

"Tom's response?" Ben paused for dramatic affect. "He said, 'These tools are for management, not for construction workers.' Tom goes on to tell me that at the end of each day his crew and construction foreman fill out a report on each segment of the project. In turn, Tom inputs this information to his management program."

That all sounded very familiar to Phillip, so he asked, "How's it working for him?"

"Not nearly as well as he had hoped. His crew feels like he's micromanaging. It doesn't help them a bit when a hammer hits a nail or a saw cuts a board. All they know is their day is longer filling out paperwork that, to them, is meaningless. As a result, the reports aren't always on time or accurate. They fill in the minimum to get by. Nothing more."

Ben looked directly at Phillip to make certain he was starting to get the point. "So I asked Tom, 'Who's actually building the home? You and your laptop, or the people at the site with their hammers, nails, and saws?'"

As a manager, Phillip could clearly see Tom's point. "He's a manager, Ben. He has a responsibility to effectively manage his projects. I don't care how much his crew complains. They need to suck it up and do what they're told."

"Ah, there's the compliance manager coming out again, Phil. I would suspect you would recommend Tom say, 'Fill out your end-of-day report or you're fired.'" Ben could see Phillip's expression begin to change. Perhaps another revelation was imminent.

"But he needs the report, Ben, so what do you recommend he do?" Phillip had been in shoes similar to Tom's and knew the challenge he faced.

"It goes back to internalization as a method of motivation, Phil. If Tom wants his crew to willingly participate and accurately fill out his end-of-day forms, the information on those forms has to be seen by the crew as a benefit to them first. Then the information Tom needs becomes a by-product of the crew doing something for themselves." Once again, Ben could see Phillip's wheels turning, then his fingers begin to type.

"So you're suggesting management tools have to be developed from the field up, right? They have to be beneficial to the people who are responsible for actually delivering the final product. In my case, sales."

"Not necessarily all management tools, Phil. Certain tools wouldn't require field participation at all. It's all about providing the right tool for the job. The point is, if Tom is trying to have impact at the job site, it's about providing tools that result in behavioral change for his crew and managers." Ben's draw took some time off his cigar. "In the case of sales transformation, the same thing applies. It's all about providing tools that result in behavioral change for your account executives and managers."

Phillip stopped typing and stared off toward the ball field. "I'm thinking about our sales force automation program. We bought it to help us manage sales. There is no doubt we've seen some benefit, but, frankly, it's been a struggle."

"And you just uncovered the problem, my friend. You bought a sales force automation program and tools like that to help you manage sales." Ben tapped the table emphatically three times to drive home his point.

"Sales cannot be managed, Phil. The sooner you figure that out, the better. Sales are the *output* of a process. By the time revenue and margins are generated, everything critical to the sale has already been done. Lead generation, prospecting, qualifying, presentations, and negotiations have occurred well before a sale ever hits your books."

"You are so right, Ben. I was a sales rep, so I should know." Once again, all Phillip could do is shake his head. "As a manager who came from the sales ranks, I should certainly know better. What happened to me?"

"Don't blame yourself, Phil. You're dealing with some things that are beyond your control." Ben reached over and patted Phillip's knee. "A sales organization's performance is typically judged by the *output* of sales revenue and margins. Their level of performance, therefore, is determined by something that can't be managed. That's why the title 'sales manager' has always bothered me. You're calling someone something that can't even be done."

Phillip chuckled at the thought of putting "sales manager" on someone's business card.

"It's starts as an obsession with numbers, my friend." Ben once again used his placemat as a prop. "So here's a management report. What's it got on it? It has lots of numbers. Look, I get it. Wall Street or our business owners are critically important, and their obsession with numbers is essential to determining our value to the market and/or equity investors. Senior management makes performance commitments to shareholders, the expectations are set, and our value rises and falls on our performance relative to those commitments and expectations. Unfortunately, that obsession and those commitments, like other things, flow downhill from executive leadership to middle management and field sales management, ultimately landing on the desks of salespeople."

Phillip leaned back and nodded his head in agreement. "My presentations to the board always include the previous period's commitments and our performance against them—all numbers. Then we move on to the forecast for the next period. Once again, all numbers."

"It happens over and over again, Phil. And as long as commitments are met, everyone, at least for the short term, is happy. But what happens if you're short of the commitment?" Ben pointed his index finger at Phillip and cocked his thumb as if it were a gun. "Well, it turns out that what flows downhill can also hit the fan. What do you think is thrown off, Phil?"

"I know exactly what's thrown off, Ben; numbers and more numbers. I can hear myself harping at my sales team after every board meeting. 'We're not at objective, so…What have you sold? How many prospects have you identified? How many new leads have you generated? How many new proposals have you submitted? What is their dollar value? What's in the pipeline?' All of it's numbers. Wow. "

"Don't be so hard on yourself," Ben said. "I understand the value of knowing where you are relative to your targets. And it has to happen. The failure, though, is the attempt to *manage* these numbers. Remember output? Sales, a proposal submitted, or the generation of a lead, are all *outputs* of processes and therefore can't be managed. Get the picture?"

Phillip lifted his hands from his keyboard and picked up his iced tea. "A picture that was as cloudy as this iced tea is becoming as clear as spring water."

"So now I'm curious, Phil." Ben held up his placemat/management report again. "When you see shortfalls in the numbers, what do you and your managers say to your salespeople?"

Phillip looked sheepish as he replied. "I say, 'Come on, guys, you need to go out and sell more' or 'You need to get more activity in the pipeline.' 'You need to find more prospects.' 'You need to generate X number of new leads this week.'"

Ben nodded along with a knowing smile as he got the exact answer he expected.

"You see, Phil, when you manage by the numbers, the primary fix to a sales shortfall is demanding more activity, more *numbers*. Well, what happens if there are people on your team who don't have all the knowledge and skills they need to convert that additional activity into sales? If they follow your instructions, you're asking them to engage in more activity they are already doing poorly."

"I'm sure I've done that on multiple occasions," Phillip admitted.

"It's not just you, Phil. It happens every day and in many companies." Ben placed his feet on the chair next to him in the exact same position that had caused them to fall asleep the day before. "The increase in activity may result in a short-term bump in sales, but you keep demanding more and more over time and you create burnout and turnover. Even if your company does multiple sales promotions to generate more activity, after a while all they promote is skepticism from wary customers expecting the next 'if you buy now' routine. Eventually the sales staff has nothing more to give and still can't meet the numbers. Then what? A new sales promotion? New salespeople? New sales management? It becomes a never-ending cycle."

"So what's the fix, Ben? Could you give me an example of what I can do?"

"Let's stay on the sales force automation example. It couldn't be a more important tool, Phil. It's unfortunate, but many companies don't get SFA's full value because of the way they use it.

"The problem starts with how decisions to implement SFA are made. Remember, the driving force behind most SFA purchase decisions is managing the sales pipeline, right?" Phillip saw the eyes that had been boring into him from across the table take a quick glance at the cigar. "Since SFA programs are somewhat costly, the decision on what system to implement and what elements to include happen at senior levels within an organization.

"And don't forget, just like my homebuilder friend, Tom, and his new software, it's a management tool. Unfortunately, just like with Tom's construction crew, it turns out the *last* thing an account executive wants to do is to work longer just to implement a new tool for managers. The truth is, they are trying to *sell* something, feed the family, pay the mortgage."

"That's true, Ben. Some of them, maybe most of them, see it as a burden, and that certainly isn't the intention."

Phillip typed another note while Ben ignored the cigar and took a sip of tea before he continued.

"Sometimes managers get frustrated with the lack of field participation and decide to make it a compliance issue, even forcing their sales team to enter certain information if they want to be paid. Sound familiar, my friend?"

"I'm guilty, Ben," Phillip admitted like in a courtroom, while raising his hand like in a classroom.

"It can become a bit of a game." Ben picked up the salt and pepper shakers and moved them as if they were pieces on a chessboard. "Salespeople enter just enough information to get a check or in just enough time to avoid a beating over questionable activity numbers. The output becomes over-inflated closing ratios because a lot of reps only enter information on sales they make or are about to make. Or just to keep management happy, some may report a bunch of activities that never took place. As a result, management doesn't get accurate reports and salespeople waste time entering minimal, and sometimes bogus, information. And both are complaining about it the entire time."

"I'm getting the problem, Ben. Now how in the heck do I fix it?" Phillip placed his hands back on his keyboard.

"Look at the first four on your sales transformation list of questions, Phil." Ben tapped the top of Phillip's laptop monitor.

Phillip already had the file open. "Let's see. All four are about developing a formal sales process the sales team takes ownership of."

Ben took his feet down from the chair next to him and leaned toward Phillip again. "The sales process is a sales tool, not a management tool. If the content of your sales force automation program is directly tied to a formal sales process that each salesperson has already taken ownership of, it also becomes a sales tool. It becomes something the *salesperson* believes they need to sell more of their products and services at higher margins, not what management needs to satisfy their thirst for reports." Ben gently patted the placemat. "Management reports should be a by-product of the information the salespeople feel is relevant to them. That way, everyone gets what they want."

"That's brilliant," Phillip almost mumbled without looking up from his fingers feverishly banging his keyboard.

With his cigar back between his fingers, Ben waved his hand next to the laptop monitor to get Phillip's attention. "I want you to get this critical point, son."

Phillip immediately stopped typing, took his hands off his keyboard, and looked directly at Ben. The older man was staring directly back at him.

"Remember, your formal sales process is intended to change the behavior of your salespeople during their customer engagements. Sales force automation becomes a tool to manage behavioral change, not just numbers. It can be used to identify gaps in behavior that lead to a sales rep's failure to perform. If you want to play with the numbers, your metrics need to align with the methodology and measure, or at least facilitate, a discussion of behavioral change, not just results."

Phillip slowly moved his hands back to his keyboard as if he hoped Ben wouldn't notice. "Is it okay if I type now, Ben? I want to make sure I capture this point."

"Absolutely, Phil. I just wanted to make certain you know how important this is." Without losing any of his intensity, Ben sat back in his chair. "With any tool you develop, you have to identify the desired impact on business results first. Then you define the ideal behaviors of both salespeople and leaders to achieve the results. As you provide them the tools, the organization has to continually measure changes in behavior and its resulting impact on performance. It'll not only help you validate the investment, but it will allow you to identify the characteristics of training, performance systems, and work environment that are actually impacting success. If a tool doesn't support the right behaviors and produce measurable results, it really isn't a tool at all."

Ben paused long enough for Phillip to stop typing and rubbed his brow.

"This thought just struck me," Phillip said. "What about marketing programs? I am trying to get that group more proactive with the sales organization."

"Now you're thinking, my friend," Ben said proudly with a nod and a smile. "To be effective and supportive, all the lead generation programs, support materials, presentation templates, product releases, have to be in concert and in alignment with the formal sales process. Everything they provide should support the desired behaviors of your salespeople. That's a great observation, Phil."

Phillip finished typing and hit enter as if it were the final note in a concert pianist's performance. "This stuff today is invaluable, Ben. As always, I can't wait to put all this in to practice."

"There is a lot here, Phil, but we are in the home stretch." Ben pointed to Phillip's laptop with his cigar. "If you're ready, we can add a few more questions to your list."

"Fire away, Ben." And Phillip was ready to type again.

Ben raised three fingers. "Here we go."

"One, is your formal sales process completely integrated with your systems such as sales force automation, customer relationship management, and any other sales and management programs?

"Two, do your systems and management tools include measurement of behavioral change and not just results?

"And finally, are your marketing programs and materials completely aligned to and in support of your sales process?"

Phillip finished typing and collapsed back in to his chair. He looked at Ben in amazement. "They didn't come close to teaching me any of this in school."

Ben reached over to the ashtray and picked up his cigar. "As Mark Twain once said, I never let school get in the way of my education."

"Amen. The only evidence of my MBA is the fact that I can calculate my own cost of capital, not only can I spell the word 'paradigm' but I actually know what one is, and I no longer have problems in my life, just issues and improvement opportunities." Phillip and Ben shared another good laugh.

As their laughter faded, Ben looked over at the ball field. "It's funny, my friend. We all have to remember that business is a social event, not a natural phenomenon. If we keep our eyes and minds open, we can find lessons everywhere, every day. As a matter of fact, we're going to have our next meeting across the street at a Little League game. I've been a fan for many years, and everything we need for the next lesson in sales transformation happens at these Little League fields over and over again, year after year."

"So you're telling me I should have been in the bleachers and not in the classroom?" Phil asked as he pointed across the street to the metal stands behind the backstop.

"You played ball at those fields, son, so you witnessed these lessons as a youngster. You were just having too much fun playing baseball to notice them." Ben reached over to the ashtray and put out his cigar, signaling the end to another lesson. "First pitch is at four tomorrow. I'll meet you at field number two."

"Can't wait, Ben." Phillip forced those words from his mouth, but it had nothing to do with his meeting with Ben the next day. It was location, location, location.

Phillip shut his eyes and took a deep breath, then continued his journey to sales transformation.

CHAPTER 9

Good Coach, Bad Coach—Lessons from a Little League Ballpark

Phillip had the pleasure of attending several world-class sporting events in his lifetime. He had been fortunate enough to go to several World Series games, two Super Bowls, a Summer Olympics, and a major golf championship or two. The night before each, he'd slept like a rock. For a Little League game with Ben, he couldn't sleep a wink. Not one.

There were layers upon layers of emotion for Phillip. He hadn't been to a Little League ball field since the day before his dad died. Phillip's last minutes alone with his father had been spent riding on his broad shoulders from the field to the car after a 10 to 8 victory at the very park where Phillip was meeting Ben.

No amount of counseling or friends begging had been able to coax him back to the place where the most vivid memories of his father were created. It was just too painful. He hadn't mentioned this to Ben, nor did he think he would. He wasn't sure why, but Ben was the only person Phillip would do this for. Maybe it was just the fatherly way Ben had spoken to him at times.

There was also a layer of emotion connected to Phillip's realization that he and Ben were nearing the end of this part of the journey to sales transformation. He knew Ben would go on to help Bill Travis conquer the world of tartar sauce while Phillip focused on transforming his organization into trusted advisors and partners to their customers. There wasn't any doubt in Phillip's mind that their friendship would continue, probably for their lifetimes, but also no doubt that it would never have the same intensity required for Ben to teach him the truth about sales transformation.

Emotions were high for Ben, too. His time with Phillip gave him a renewed sense of purpose. He felt re-awakened—alive and useful again. While over the years Ben had run his sales organizations based on the truths he now shared with Phillip, he had never given them to anyone else. He had never even written them down. The truths were recorded now, in 1's and 0's on a laptop hard drive. From there, they would live through Phillip to do what they were intended to do, and that's impact other people's lives.

Ben knew it was almost time to let Phillip go. He had passed on what he knew to be true, and now the younger student and his organization had to execute in order to transform the sales organization the way they all wanted. The final lessons would be the most critical, the areas where many organizations failed to achieve total transformation. Ben hoped the setting wouldn't be too distracting, but he couldn't think of a better place or way to share this story.

It was a beautiful early fall day. You couldn't call it a nip in the air, but a ten-degree drop from the steamy summer highs was enough to make people want to cook some gumbo and throw a log on the fire. Ben couldn't wait to get to the park. As usual, he arrived fifteen minutes before the scheduled game time and got a seat directly behind home plate with a clear view of both dugouts. He had chosen this particular game because he knew both coaches and knew Phillip could see the differences in how each approached his responsibilities.

For the first time since their initial meeting at the café, Phillip didn't arrive early, at least to the field. *How could a 39-year-old, C-level executive, responsible for managing hundreds of mature adults generating millions of dollars in sales be on the verge of hyperventilating in his car at the parking lot of a Little League ball field?* Phillip had to let go of his anxiety. If he followed the advice of his counselors, he had to embrace and accept his loss and love the part of him that felt the pain. Phillip was certain it would never go away.

It was time to move on, though, to take another step. Fate had brought him to Ben, or Ben to him. Maybe it was both. All Phillip knew was that he was a better man because of it, and in the words of his father, every day was new, every day presented new opportunities to do right, be right. Phillip had an obligation to his people, his company, his customers, Ben, and, yes, to his dad, to continually find ways to impact people's lives in meaningful, measurable ways. He had to believe that every step closer to Ben and the ball field was a step closer to realizing that potential.

Phillip Evan Hawthorne grabbed his notepad and pen, opened his car door, stood, faced field number two, and continued his journey to sales transformation.

"Steeeerrrriiiike" was the call as Phillip approached the stands. He was amazed at how little things had changed. That was the beauty of America's pastime and the continuum of life. Pre-pubescent boys with high-pitched voices, were cheered on by parents, mostly moms, in folding chairs divided by teams along each baseline. The fields themselves were mixtures of dusty clay with patches of grass that made them only vaguely resemble the baseball fields folks watched on television. And there was the nearly constant chatter of "Hey, batta, batta, batta...SWING!" through every pitch on all four fields.

Ben waved Phillip over and patted the space on the metal bench next to him before standing up. "If you're wondering how I got these seats, let's just say I've got connections. They come with good news and bad news, though."

"The bad news first, please. I want to end on a positive." Phillip and Ben exchanged a hug that was quicker than their usual, then Phillip dropped into the seat next to Ben as he'd been directed.

"The bad news is we're in the no smoking section. It actually extends all the way to the parking lot, so I'll have no timer as long as we're here." Ben patted his empty shirt pocket that normally held his cigar.

"That may be bad news to you, but I couldn't be happier," Phillip said with a wide grin. "I spend half our time together trying to figure out how many puffs are left in your stories. With listening and taking notes, it's exhausting."

Ben put his arm around Phillip's shoulder and said, "Then it's all good news for you, my friend. Our game clock is turned off today. Let's play ball!"

Phillip surveyed the field and tried to figure out what Ben would have him look for. The scoreboard? The umpire? A third base coach? The kid in the batter's box? What additional truths about sales transformation would he learn at a Little League game?

Ben leaned over and spoke to Phillip at a volume barely above a whisper. "These stands have ears, so you'll have to listen closely, at least at first. I'm here often and have been for years. I know a lot of these parents, their kids, and coaches, and I don't want to ever be banned from my favorite ballpark."

"Is Ben Delaney about to gossip?" Phillip whispered back.

"Nope. I'm just going to share some observations that may bother some folks. No gossip. Just truth. But sometimes the truth hurts." Ben tapped Phillip's left knee with the back of his right hand and nodded toward the dugout on their left. "See the coach sitting on the end of the bench, the one talking on his cell phone? That's

Dillon Porter." Then Ben turned his head to the right and nodded toward the first base dugout. "The coach kneeling down next to the batter on deck is Cullen Joseph."

"Good coaches?" Phillip asked while looking back and forth at each of the men.

"One great, one not so good. Don't get me wrong. They're both fine men. Besides that, the only other thing they have in common is they both want to win. One knows how to do it, the other doesn't.

"Good swing, batter!" Ben yelled as the player at the plate hit a solid, but slightly foul, line drive down the left field line. "He got a little in front of that one."

Phillip smiled at the thought of Ben sitting here at the ball games shouting out encouragement to kids he probably didn't know. "So tell me how these two guys approach the game differently. What makes one great and the other not so good, Mr. Ben?" Phillip picked his pad up from the bench next to him and placed it on his lap. For a moment, he felt like a sportswriter doing an interview.

"Okay, the guy down third base, Dillon? You know why he coaches?" Ben looked around to see if anyone was listening.

Phillip glanced over to the left and saw Coach Dillon with his phone still glued to his ear. "Well, it appears it gives him time to return calls."

"No, he's not always on the phone. The fact that he is at all, though, tells you he's not paying attention to what's happening with the boys and the game." Ben shook his head as he watched Coach Dillon talk with his free hand, too, while his pitcher threw ball four and put runners on first and second.

"Actually, the reason Dillon coaches is to make sure his son, he's number nineteen playing second, gets to play every game. I bet you saw that when you were playing ball, Phil." Ben glanced at

Phillip and saw him nodding in memory. "Okay, I'm sure that's not the only reason, but I doubt his son would be starting if Dillon wasn't the coach."

"Yep. I played on a team with a coach just like Dillon," Phillip said as the umpire called ball one on the next batter. "It seemed to bother the parents a whole lot more than it bothered the kids. We were just having fun. I remember our parents hating it, though."

"It helps if a dad like Dillon also happens to be a good coach and his son a good player. Then, pretty much nobody cares. It's all for the good of the team." Ben let out a hoot and clapped as the pitcher threw a strike on the inside corner. "Nice pitch!"

"So what, in your opinion, Ben, makes a good coach?" Phillip asked as he picked up his pen.

"Since you're a guy who likes to end on a positive note, let's talk about the not-so-good coach first," Ben said, pointing to the dug-out on the left. "Dillon's son, like many players on his team, is not a very good ballplayer. He doesn't have the knowledge or the skills to play and win. But do me a favor and take a look. He's playing second base. Notice anything about him?"

Phillip looked toward second. "Well, for one, he is spotlessly clean. Is that what you're talking about?"

"That's probably because he doesn't know how to slide," Ben said with a slight chuckle. "But it's more than that. See his glove? It's new and the best made. Same with his cleats. When you see his bat, you'll notice the same thing. That's a problem."

"Oh, come on, Ben," Phillip said as he turned his head away from the game and toward Ben. "What's wrong with a dad buying the best stuff for his kid? I can totally relate to him wanting his children playing with the best equipment he can buy."

"I could, too, if his son knew how to use it," Ben said as he clapped for a called strike. "Remember, I said Dillon's son didn't have the knowledge and skill to play the game. Dillon thinks that his son's play will improve if he has better equipment, and that just ain't true. I mean, look at the kid."

Phillip looked down instead and shook his head. "You have no idea how much money I've wasted on new golf clubs thinking they would improve my game. It never happens."

"It actually goes a step farther with Dillon. He knows his kid can't hit, field, or throw. So not only has he bought new equipment, he also sent him to a baseball clinic this past spring." Ben's head flinched as a foul ball slammed into the backstop. There was no reaction from Phillip as his eyes continued to focus on Coach Dillon.

Phillip leaned over, placed his elbows on his knees, and rested his chin on his fists. "Okay, I get your point about Coach Dillon buying expensive equipment. But what's the problem with a dad sending his kid to a sports camp?"

"Nothing at all. I've got no problem with a kid going to a clinic. It's what happens when they come back. If a coach isn't prepared to reinforce the knowledge and skills the kid gained while at the clinic, most likely it won't stick." Ben nodded back toward Coach Dillon again. "I think Dillon may have played some sandlot ball with friends as a youngster, but other than that, he's had no exposure. He doesn't even understand the fundamentals of the game."

Phillip turned his attention to his right where Coach Cullen was behind one of his young players demonstrating how to step into a swing. "So what's this guy's story?" Phillip asked as he pointed his thumb toward the right dugout.

"Coach Cullen doesn't have a kid of his own on the team. His two boys played for him years ago, but they're grown now, one in college, another married with a kid. Coaching stayed in Cullen's blood, so he kept on doing it even after his kids left." Ben grabbed a pack of gum from his pants pocket. "You want a chew, Phil?"

"Sure, Ben, thanks," Phillip said as he pulled a stick from the pack. "My dad used to buy baseball cards for me from the concession stand on game day. The gum was always rock hard, really brittle, and the flavor lasted for about ten seconds, but to get to the cards, I'd keep cramming that gum in my mouth until I couldn't hold any more."

"Those are great memories, my friend. I'd do the same as a kid and pretend it was chewing tobacco." Ben stuck his piece of Juicy Fruit between his cheek and gums.

"Anyway," Ben continued, "Coach Cullen's the kind of guy you want your kids to play for. He not only produces winning teams, but several of his players have gone on to play ball in high school and college. He's even coached a couple who turned pro."

"So he doesn't have any of his own kids on the team. Is that what makes him better?" Phillip gave Ben a quizzical look.

"Not at all. Cullen is the same coach today that he was when his own kids were on the field. It doesn't matter a lick to him. He knows what he's doing." Ben looked over to the scoreboard in centerfield that showed a three-run lead for Coach Cullen's team in the top of the first. "See that score? It'll be far more lopsided when this thing is over.

"The funny thing is, Phil, Cullen's players come to him starting out with pretty much the same level of skills Coach Dillon's do. By the end of the season, Coach Cullen's in the playoffs and Coach Dillon is finished coaching for the year and out buying the latest equipment."

"I get that Cullen is better, Ben. You and the score are making that perfectly clear." Phillip had been holding his pen poised over his pad for two or three minutes, ready but unsure of what to write. "I'm looking for what he actually does that makes him a more effective coach. How's he different?"

"Okay, Phil, if you really want to put that pen to paper, now's the time," Ben said as he looked down at Phillip's still-blank writing pad. Then the old man went into pure teaching mode again.

"Let's talk about you for a moment, Coach Phillip. You or your managers meet with your folks before a new sales year begins. When it comes to a discussion of numbers, what do you guys talk about?"

"You know how tough that is," Phillip said. "You've been there before, my man. Our numbers get more aggressive every year, so rolling out revenue objectives gets a little harder every time. It's not a very happy occasion. It is, though, a pretty simple conversation. We break the sales numbers down by the month and figure each rep has to keep a minimum of four times that monthly revenue target in their proposal pipeline. Then we ask them to submit a plan as to how they're going to get it done." Phillip leaned back and held his hands in front of him, palms up, as if he were saying, "That's it." "We give them a couple of weeks to submit the plan, then we're all off and running."

"Got it, Coach Phil. So what types of things do you typically see in their plans?" Ben asked. Ben pulled out another stick of gum and popped it into his cheek, baseball-style.

"It's pretty typical stuff," Phillip admitted. "They tell us what they plan to close in the short term, stuff they're already working on. Then they tell us what customers they plan to approach with what new products and services in the longer term and talk about what they plan to close. Sometimes they'll bring a list of customers coming up for service contract renewal and give us the revenue they expect from that. We'll talk about what they believe is coming up for bid in the next six to twelve months and the revenue they expect to get from RFPs. That's about it."

"Interesting," Ben said without looking at Phillip. "So it's kind of like Coach Cullen saying to his players, 'We need to score fourteen runs to win this game,' and his players responding, 'Okay, we'll plan to score two runs in the first inning, two runs in the second. Then longer term, we're planning to score four in the third and then six in the fourth inning." Ben slowly turned his head toward Phillip and deadpanned, "That about right?"

Phillip let out a hardy laugh. "I swear, I have never thought of it that way, but that's exactly what it's like. It's so funny when you put it like that."

"So what happens if your team doesn't hit one of their commitments to score? What happens if they fall short of a revenue target?" Ben asked, turning back to watch the game.

"We tell them they have to score more, close more, in the next inning, the next month," Phillip said as he put his chin back in its resting place on the palms of his hands.

"And there, my friend, is the problem," Ben said as he patted Phillip's knee again. "You begin to realize how impossible it is to hold someone accountable for a sales number. A good coach has to hold people accountable for doing the things that produce the number. The end result of runs for Cullen's team or revenue for your team becomes a byproduct of people doing the right things in the right way."

Phillip picked up his pad and started writing.

"I'm telling you, son. A lot of what you need to know is right here at the ballpark. Just keep watching, keep observing," Ben said as his gaze went from baseline to baseline and back again.

"The first practice of the year, what do you think Cullen does?" Ben asked, pointing his head toward first.

"I would say he starts with some sort of practice drills, working on the fundamentals. Probably some batting practice, maybe let the boys shag some fly balls, hit a few grounders to the infield." Phillip recalled his first practices each season as a kid.

"Nope. Coach Cullen doesn't even have the boys bring their equipment to the first practice. He sits them down and talks about their individual goals for the season. They all say they want to win the championship and make the all-star team, but he talks to each one about what they want to accomplish individually as players." Not unlike a salty, old-school baseball coach, Ben spat on the ground in front of the bleachers.

"You know, sales and baseball both have numbers, Phil. To get to the championship, it's the number of wins and losses. Shoot, two numbers determine the outcome of a game; one team's runs against the other's. But to get to wins and championships, a variety of numbers come in to play. You've got batting average, earned run average, on-base percentage, number of stolen bases, errors, and assists as examples. It's coaching the behavior that causes those numbers to happen, driving some higher and others lower, that produces a winning team."

Phillip tried to mentally translate Ben's words into business terms as he wrote nearly word for word what he was saying. He really missed his laptop. "So how does this relate to our managers, Ben?"

"There actually is a formula for what you do, Phil," Ben said as he rubbed his hands together as if he were about to grab the handle of a bat. "Ready? Activity times proficiency equals sales. Remember, sales are the output of the formula, and it's impossible to manage, just like it's impossible for Coach Cullen to manage runs. So to be an effective manager and coach, you have to look at the metrics for activity and proficiency and work with both, just like Cullen works with batting average and ERA."

Ben held up two fingers. "For activity, you've got two metrics: the number of new opportunities and the number of proposals. For proficiency you have three." Then he held up three fingers. "Closing ratio, average sale value, and proposal ratio."

That made sense to Phillip.

"I want you to think about your demand that all of your sales reps keep four times their quota in their sales pipeline," Ben said. "You see any potential problems with that?"

"It works out okay for us. We just figured we close about one out of four deals we propose, so mathematically it made sense," Phillip said as he leaned back on the bench behind him. "Do *you* see problems with it?"

"Well, if everyone were exactly average and closed exactly one out of four deals, you'd be right on, but look out there on the field. Can Coach Cullen expect all his players to finish the season with the same batting average? Can Coach Phil expect *his* players to do it?"

"Nope. Some will have a higher batting average and some lower, just like some of my reps will close a lot higher percentage of their deals and some a lower percentage." Phillip started writing another note.

"Okay, now we're getting to what a good coach does at the beginning of a season, or the beginning of a sales year." Ben smiled as he looked down the first base line to Coach Cullen. "A good coach looks at each player's metrics and customizes a plan just for that player. What is their closing ratio now and where does it need to be? Based on their individual skill level, how many new opportunities do they have to uncover to hit their number? How many new proposals do they have to generate from those opportunities? Some people may need five times their revenue target in proposals, some just three.

"Based on the metrics, each player's plan will be a little different. But the plan becomes more than just hitting a final sales number or final score. It's focused on changing the behaviors that impact activity and proficiency. Make sense?"

"Absolute sense, Ben, just like everything you've taught me. The final score is the result of setting goals early and working on the incremental improvements needed to reach them. That's how a coach wins." Phillip added the note "Clearly define goals for activity and proficiency" to his list of revelations.

Phillip completely forgot he was at a ball game until he heard a father in the stands behind him yell, "Get ready for a bunt!" Phillip looked up from his notes just in time to see a batter square off for a bunt, take a semi-swing, and hit a soft line drive toward second. Unfortunately for him, the second baseman didn't have to take so much as a step to catch the ball in the air and promptly tag out the runner who was headed from first to second to complete a double play.

Ben poked Phillip with his elbow and let out a little laugh. "Did you see that bunt? I mean it looked like he squared up for a sacrifice bunt, just like he should. I don't know what the heck it was after that. Anyway, there was a good example of a gap in behavior that affected a kid's batting average and, at least potentially, the final score of the game. Something as seemingly insignificant and easy-looking as a bunt may have cost his team the game."

"That's true. And from the looks of the score, they really, really needed to advance that runner," Phillip said as he looked at the scoreboard.

"Yeah, no kidding." Ben glanced over at Coach Dillon's bench. "So here's an excellent opportunity to discuss the second thing a good coach does once they've set goals. The batter needs help, right?" Ben didn't even slow down for Phillip's response. "So here's what a good coach would do. Let's say one of the batter's goals was to increase their batting average. If he had successfully executed the sacrifice bunt, the out wouldn't have counted against his average. On top of that, his behavior caused the runner to be tagged out on his way to second, so it was a double whammy. The coach just saw a gap in his *behavior* that caused that outcome."

"So the gap wasn't the fact he was out," Phillip said, "or that he failed to advance the runner. The gap was his failure to execute the bunt, right?"

"Exactly. A lot the sales managers identify a gap in sales rep's performance as the difference between a sales revenue number that was committed to and the number that was actually achieved." To emphasize his point, Ben slapped Phillip's knee as he spoke. "That just ain't right. Missing the number isn't the problem - it's the rep's behavior, their execution.

"C'mon, son, you remember what it was like. If you missed a revenue target when you were a rep, you didn't need a coach to tell you missed it, just like that boy didn't need a coach to tell him he bunted into a double play. The kid was there. He saw it all happen. He needs a coach to help him understand *why* it happened. That's what'll lower the chance it happens again."

"Good point, Ben. You're so right." Phillip recognized the familiar feeling of another arriving revelation.

"So goals have been set and gaps identified, Phil. The next thing a good coach has to do is to figure out what caused the failure. Was the player not committed to bunting? Did he not know how to position his feet after the pitch or hold the bat? Or did he know what he was supposed to do but hadn't practiced the skill enough to pull it off? Those are the questions a good coach has to answer. To fix the problem, he's got to know what caused it."

"So let me see if I get this," Phillip said, continuing to write as fast as he could. "It sounds like you're saying there are three reasons someone could fail: commitment, knowledge, or skill. Is that right?"

"No, Phil, there are actually five, but the other two probably wouldn't apply to this bunter," Ben said as he nodded toward the bench. "The environment could have come into play, but I don't think the sun got in the batter's eyes. Or another possible reason for failure is capacity. Let's say the boy wasn't exactly the sharpest tool in the shed and could never understand bunting, or he didn't have the physical strength to lift a bat. The lack of capacity could also cause someone to fail."

"So it's environment, capacity, commitment, knowledge, and skills, correct?" Phillip asked while checking his notes.

"Exactly, Phil. Those are all of the root causes for failure. As a manager, you have an obligation to work on removing or mitigating environmental problems, and hopefully you are hiring people who have the capacity to do their jobs. So you're really working with commitment, knowledge, and skills," Ben said as he pointed to each of those words on Phillip's notepad. "Those are root causes you can really help someone with."

"Excellent, Ben. So I've got setting goals, finding gaps in behavior, and figuring out the cause of the gap. What's next?" Phillip asked as he raised his pen.

"Next is prescribing fixes. A good coach has to be able to tell a player what to do to get better. He can't just say, 'You gotta do better,' and hope the player finds a way. A good coach knows what resources are available to correct problems with commitment, skill, or knowledge." Ben intermittently watched the ballgame while also reading what Phillip was writing in his notes.

As soon as Phillip stopped writing, he put down his pen. "I can see where that would be a challenge for someone like Coach Dillon. If he doesn't know the fundamentals of the game, how could he recognize what was wrong and tell someone how to get better?" Phillip looked down the first base line to Coach Cullen. "So where did Cullen get his training? Was it trial and error? Was he a ballplayer?"

"Before I tell you, I have a question. Are all your managers going through the training for your sales process? Are they attending the same sessions as your reps?" Ben was pretty certain he already knew the answer.

Phillip turned to Ben with a knowing grin of his own. "Okay, Ben. I've gotten to the point where I recognize the times you're setting me up. This is one of them. Some of my field sales managers may go to the sessions, but you can be certain anyone above that level hasn't or won't. I think the opinion is that this is training for sales-people, not for managers."

"Well, let's talk about Cullen for a minute, because it's a funny thing, Phil," Ben said as he scratched his head just above his left ear. "Cullen didn't play baseball at all as a kid. He would watch a game every now and then on TV, but fancied himself more of a hoops player. Played high school basketball. He didn't actually play baseball before he started coaching it."

"You're kidding," Phillip said with a respectful glance in the direction of Coach Cullen Joseph. "So how'd he learn to be such a good baseball coach?"

"Remember I told you Coach Dillon sent his boy to clinics?" Ben nodded toward Dillon Porter.

"Yep." Phillip nodded in return.

"Well, so did Coach Cullen, except he went to the camps with his kids. I mean, he couldn't actually participate, but he watched and learned. He figured if he was going to reinforce what his boys were being taught, he better know what they knew, see what they saw." Just like a batter in the box, Ben stomped his feet on the foot rail to knock some dirt off.

"You see, Phil, the best coaches know what to look for. They can see problems in a swing or stance. They can help figure out what's wrong and what to do to fix it. They're always evaluating their play-er's performance and helping them improve, always helping them get better." Ben jumped up, pumped his fist in the air and let out a yell as a batter doubled to right field. "Way to go, batter!"

"So you're saying my management should be going through training?" Phillip asked with resignation.

"Should Coach Dillon go to baseball camps?" Ben asked with his head cocked and his eyebrows raised.

"Duh," Phillip said while displaying what could have been the goofiest look ever displayed by a C-level executive. Maybe not, but it was close. "So I've got goals, gaps, root causes for failure, and fixes. Anything else to add to the list?"

"Yep, one more thing. The last thing a good coach does is to evaluate the player's performance the next time he bunts to make certain improvement is happening. Is he committed to bunting when the coach gives him the signal?" Ben asked as he nodded toward the third base coach. "Does he show he has the knowledge to bunt by squaring properly and holding the bat right? Does he demonstrate the skill to bunt by pushing the ball down and getting it to roll about ten feet out and within the baselines? If he does, the corrective action worked. If those things don't happen, there's more that needs to be done to change his behavior."

"So now I see five steps in this management process," Phillip said. "Setting goals, exposing gaps in performance, figuring out the root causes for failure, determining what needs to be done to fix the problem, then evaluating performance. It's like a continuum, isn't it?"

"Yes, it is, son. If your managers apply it, they'll make the transition from being a lousy Coach Dillon to an effective Coach Cullen. It will be *the* difference when it comes to sales transformation."

"I'm starting to get it, Ben." Phillip looked down at his notes, then over to Coach Cullen. "Our managers have to be better coaches."

"That's exactly right, Phil. The key to a successful sales transformation will be how it's managed." Ben reached over and tapped Phillip's note pad. Phillip grabbed his pen.

"The real impact from what we've been talking about will only happen when sellers and managers all get better at what they do. Just like Coach Dillon, some companies rely on classroom learning by itself when there just isn't enough time to get it done in the short time the students are there. These little baseball camps, just like most sales training, last for a couple of days. I heard Coach Dillon yell at his boy last week, 'Come on, Bobby, you just got back from batting camp and I brought you that brand new bat. Why can't you hit that pitch?'"

Phillip gave Ben his guilty look again. "I'm not joking, Ben. I've heard my managers say 'We sent you to training. We bought you new laptops and software. Now where are the results?'"

Ben looked at the sky and shook his head as if asking "Why?" Phillip looked up at the sky and shook his head right along with Ben.

"The truth is," Ben continued, "changing people's behavior and getting them better at what they do won't happen from attending one baseball camp or a few training sessions. It'll come with different skills at different times for different people, different players. Managers as coaches, even the senior people, have to be able to spot problems in a player's game and help them improve. Your managers have to assess and support improvement day after day for each individual seller and manager that report up the chain.

"You're not gonna get anywhere near the return you could by just a handful of people changing, Phil. Just like one player on either of these teams getting better isn't going to win either one of them a championship. It'll happen when the majority not only commit to doing what it takes, but when they're held accountable for doing the things it takes to win. Doing the fundamentals the right way."

Phillip turned, looked Ben squarely in the eye, and said, "Working with kids is easy. Adults believe they already know how to play the game. Coaching them is way more difficult. I think that's the real challenge."

Ben patted Phillip on the knee again. "Sales transformation isn't for the weak of heart, my friend. It takes strong management, strong coaches that are committed to change. Accountability at every level has to be your focus. If your managers don't hold your people accountable, you'll never transform anything."

"I know it's not enough, Ben, but we've at least tried to hold them accountable. I mean every manager and rep commits to their number every month, and the compensation program penalizes them if they don't hit it."

"Phillip, Phillip, Phillip," Ben said in the most fatherly way possible, "the definition of accountability is 'responsibility to someone for some action.' The definition does not say 'responsibility for some result or some number.' Results don't happen or goals aren't reached unless people do the things they need to do to make them happen. You wouldn't believe how many sales organizations can't transform because managers either don't know how or just don't want to drive the behaviors or actions that cause results to happen. Managers who can't coach are the weak link that can cause everything we've been talking about to fall apart."

"So that takes care of my field level managers, Ben, but what about me?" Phillip asked pointedly. "What about the rest of our senior management team?"

"So far, Phil, everything we've talked about has been what you're going to get others in your organization to do. Now it's your turn. You didn't think you and the rest of your senior leadership team would come out of this unscathed, did you?"

"I was hoping," Phillip said sheepishly.

"Well, hope didn't do you much good this time around, Phil," Ben said with one of big smiles. "You know I'm going to start the next part of our conversation with a question. Are you ready?"

"As ready as I as can be," Phillip said with his head down, his eyes closed and a deep sigh.

Ben turned his body toward Phillip. "All of the company's senior management agreed sales transformation was necessary and approved the budget to get it done. I'm curious. What have they done since?"

"They've done what senior managers should do. They've talked it up, but they've also asked about and looked for results. Is there more they should do?" Phillip wanted to make certain he truly understood what Ben was about to say, so he put his pen down and looked directly at him.

"Just like other managers in your organization, senior leaders have big responsibilities when it comes to sales transformation. As a matter of fact, senior leaders' lack of support can kill the effort. The company will show a real commitment to sales transformation when you and all the other senior folks don't just acknowledge the requirement to change, but actually experience the change with the rest of the organization," Ben said.

"Senior leaders who don't change their own tune have kept a bunch of organizations from fully realizing transformation. True sales transformation doesn't happen when an individual on a team assumes the role of a trusted partner. That likely has already happened many times with a lot of your salespeople and customers. It happens when your entire company assumes that role. A company can't be a real partner unless people at the most senior levels understand the formal sales process, set the example, and hold everyone in the organization accountable for transformation."

"You do this every time, Ben. You tell me we have to change, and I have to drag out of you what and how to change. I'm begging you to hit me over the head with it," Phillip said, pounding his fist on the top of his head.

"You don't have to drag anything out of me or ask me to hit you over the head, Phil. You just have to be patient. My stories can only come how they come. It's the way I learned them."

"Point taken," Phillip responded.

"So now it's about you and all the other senior folks in your organization. Just like Coach Cullen and your field level managers, you have to attend the training that defines the selling process and coaching behaviors. You should witness the buy-in of all your people and leverage it later when you're working with sellers and managers. If you don't, how could you understand the key methodologies and be able to inspect them when you talk with your folks? You'd be a Coach Dillon, for heaven's sake."

"Looks like it's back to the sales classroom for my entire senior team." Phillip continued writing his notes.

"It's not just the sales classroom, Phil. You want your senior leaders to set the example. If you're teaching field-level managers how to be effective coaches, it would make sense for your senior leadership to do the same. Stuff flows downhill. They need to manage the people who report directly to them just like they expect their field-level people to manage theirs. They need to able to be able to properly examine and evaluate the behaviors of people in the organization to ensure the right things are happening."

"Yeah, that's right again, Ben. Senior leadership has to walk the walk," Phillip said while writing his notes.

"Not only do they have to walk the walk, they've got to be cheerleaders for everything you are doing with sales transformation. They should continually be looking for and reporting successes. They need to be blasting news about positive changes and results every chance they get.

"And you know what else?" Ben once again continued without Phillip's response. "To have trusted partnerships you have to find as many ways as you can to actually be a better partner. You and your senior leaders should be pushing everyone to find ways to serve your customers best. As an example, you could ask each department in your company to submit one new idea every month of how they could better serve your customers. That should be a huge part of your culture."

As if on cue, Ben and Phillip heard the umpire signal the end of the game on the Little League ten-run rule. The score was fourteen to four in favor of Coach Cullen's team. "Need I say any more about the impact a coach can have on his team?" Ben held out his hand out for a discreet low-five. Phillip gave it a solid slap with his left.

As the coaches, players, and parents began to pack up and leave the park, Ben held up his fingers and asked, "Are you ready for your questions?"

"Have you ever known me not to be ready?" Phillip said as he prepared to write.

"Not yet, my friend," Ben said. "So let's do it. There are seven questions today.

"First, have all managers, including senior leaders, attended training and fully committed to your formal sales process and management methodology?

"Second, have you and your managers clearly defined activity and proficiency metrics for every individual on your sales team?

"Third, do your managers consistently review those metrics to uncover gaps in performance?

"Fourth, do your managers, from field-level to C-level, hold themselves and everyone on their team accountable for the required changes in behavior?"

Once again, Ben raised his thumb. "Fifth, can senior managers effectively examine and evaluate the behaviors of people in your organization to ensure the required behavioral changes are actually taking place?"

Out of fingers, Ben started over with his pinky. "Sixth, do your senior managers actively seek and report successes with sales transformation?

Then to his ring finger again. "And seventh, are your senior managers creating programs that encourage everyone in the organization to find ways to be the best partner for your customers?"

Phillip wrote the last question slowly. As a matter of fact, the closer he got to writing the question mark, the slower he wrote. Without his cigar to tell Ben went to stop, Phillip wanted to keep him there as long as possible. He was afraid for it to end. Finally he had to ask.

"That's not all, is it?" Phillip asked hopefully.

Ben didn't respond to Phillip's question. Instead, he slowly stood and stared toward the fence in center field. The kids and coaches were gone, but through some of the taller grass by the chain links, Ben could see what looked to be the dirty white cover of a baseball.

"That's always bothered me," Ben said as he squinted to make certain he was looking at a ball.

"What are you looking at?" Phillip asked as he looked at Ben then out to center field and back at Ben again.

"A body at rest will remain at rest unless an outside force acts on it," Ben replied without looking at Phillip. "I just can't let that ball sit there."

"Okay, Mr. Newton," Phillip said. "I take it we are done with our lesson today."

Ben hopped down from the stands and headed around the backstop toward the center field fence. As he neared the third base line, he stopped and turned to Phillip. "Yes, we're done for today, but there is one more thing."

"What is it?" Phillip picked up his pad and pen.

"Sir Isaac wasn't in sales, but we can still learn from him," Ben said over his shoulder as he continued walking to the ball. "Can we meet at the café tomorrow at three?"

Phillip stood. All he could do was look at Ben and shake his head. "I wouldn't miss it, my friend."

"So Sir Isaac Newton is a part of my final lesson. Who would have thought?" Phillip said to himself as he walked toward his car and continued his journey to sales transformation.

CHAPTER 10

Paying it Forward—Isaac Newton, a Baseball, and a Cigar-Cutter

On the way home from the baseball field, Ben stopped by a gift shop and bought some wrapping paper, two gold bows, and two boxes just big enough to hold Phillip's last lesson in sales transformation. Phillip might discard the wrapping paper, the bows, maybe the boxes, but as Ben headed to their final meeting, he hoped the young CSO would hold on to at least one of his gifts until it was time for him to pass it on.

Phillip had met Ben at the café several times. He was usually anxious, but not once had he been nervous. Today was different. Ben had told him there was one more thing Phillip needed to learn. Phillip knew that meant the next meeting would be the last of the lessons about sales transformation from Ben and couldn't help but wonder about how that would change their relationship.

Plus, if there was just one more thing, why couldn't Ben have just told him in the stands at the ballpark? Maybe Ben just wanted him to think about Sir Isaac for a while, like he did with his parting lines at the end of all their other meetings. But this time it felt different.

Phillip arrived at the café forty-five minutes early. Ben was already there waiting. Phillip saw what he expected to see in front of Ben: a glass of iced tea, an ashtray, a lighter, and a Montecristo. He didn't expect to see exactly the same on the table in front of his chair. In perfect symmetrical alignment, Ben had placed iced tea, an ashtray, a Montecristo, and a lighter. But sitting between Phillip's cigar and the ashtray were two small boxes, one rectangular and about the size you would expect from a jewelry store, the other a little larger and perfectly square, both tied with gold bows.

"Aw, Ben. This one looks like a jewelry box," Phillip said with a sarcastic smile as he picked up the smaller of the two boxes. "You really shouldn't have, big guy. I'm already taken."

"The only jewelry you'd get from me would come from a Cracker Jack box, and I wouldn't bother wrapping it." Ben's smile faded quickly, and he added, "What's in that box is more special than any jewelry I could ever give you."

Ben pointed at the larger box. "Open that one first."

Phillip smiled as he reached for his present, but it was a nervous smile. He slowly tugged at the gold ribbon until it fell off the package and gently pulled away the wrapping paper. As Ben watched intently, Phillip opened the top and looked inside. It was a brand new, cork center, wool wound, Little League baseball.

"Wow, Ben. From the looks of it, this isn't the baseball you collected from center field last night is it? This looks new," Phillip said as he laid the index and middle fingers of his right hand on the ball's seams as if he were about to throw a curveball.

"No, son. The ball I picked up yesterday afternoon is on the front seat of my car and will be put back in motion at field three across the street as soon as we're done here." Ben punctuated his statement with a wink. "It served the boys well in the game and served me well as a reminder."

"It reminded you of Sir Isaac Newton's laws of motion, right?" Phillip asked as he tossed the bright white baseball back and forth from hand to hand.

Ben smiled. "When I saw the ball, I thought of the game, meeting you, Isaac Newton, sales transformation, your sales organization, then getting that ball back to where it could do what it was made to do, all in that order."

"I didn't even notice the ball yesterday," Phillip said as he stopped tossing his new prized possession and placed it on the table.

"As Sir Isaac would say, a mind at rest..." Ben looked at the ball, then quickly to Phillip.

"Ouch," Phillip said as he winced. "My mind's not at rest, it just doesn't wander to as many places as yours seems to, Ben."

"My mind's not wandering, my friend. It may take a different road than some, but there is almost always a reason it chooses the route that it does," Ben said as he reached for the smaller box and pushed it toward Phillip.

Phillip picked up the small box, held it in front of him, and looked at it closely. "I can't think of any baseball equipment that would fit in a box this small."

"Today isn't all about baseball, son," Ben said as he leaned back in his chair. "Open it."

Phillip unwrapped this box much faster. He looked to Ben more like an anxious kid tearing into a package at Christmas than a CSO preparing for a lesson on sales transformation. His rapid motions came to a grinding halt when he lifted the lid to the small box. What he saw wasn't shiny like jewelry. It was antique, well worn, battered, and had lost its shine decades before. It was Ben's old cigar cutter.

Phillip removed the cutter from its box, said nothing, then cocked his head and offered Ben a quizzical look.

"I want you to hold onto that while we talk today. I know it means little to you now, but it'll mean a whole lot more by the time we leave," Ben said with his knowing smile.

"It already means something to me, Ben, because it's yours."

"It hasn't always been mine," Ben said.

"Well, it looks like it's been around. Obviously, a cigar smoker like you needs something newer." Phillip reached down and picked up the cigar in front of him. "Are you expecting me to smoke this thing?"

"I figured this was a special occasion and you might indulge me just this once," Ben said with a huge smile.

"Okay, Ben. I will just for you," Phillip said as he picked up Ben's old, and his new, cigar cutter. "Does this thing come with an instruction manual?"

"I'll give you a lesson on how to use it, but I don't want your mind racing trying to figure out what it means for sales transformation. Right now, there's no cigar burning," Ben reminded him. "All it means is you'll know how to use it to cut a cigar."

The lesson on cutting went quickly. Both men smiled as Ben held the lighter to the end of Phillip's cigar.

"This brings back memories, son," Ben said as Phillip took his first two shallow draws and started hacking and coughing. "I was at this very café having the same violent reaction during my introduction to a Montecristo many, many years ago. Here, take a sip of this," Ben said as he slid a glass of tea across the table toward Phillip.

Phillip held his arm out to block Ben's hand and the glass as he tried to catch his breath. "This is going to take some time," Phillip said hoarsely as he wiped his eyes with a napkin.

"I think I told you when we first met in Bill's backyard that I wasn't a smoker," Ben said as he took his traditional three quick puffs.

"I should have reminded you that being a non-smoker means you don't inhale. Ever."

"That would have been a good lesson to teach me before you helped me light this thing, Ben," Phillip said with a raspy chuckle.

"I can only do so many lessons in a day, bud. And I kinda knew you would learn that one pretty quickly on your own." Ben took the napkin from under his tea and handed it to Phillip. "Here. You may need this in case you're a slower learner than I thought."

"Very funny, Ben." With his right hand, Phillip placed his now-lit cigar in the ashtray in front of him, cleared a space on the table, and opened his laptop, all while he continued to hold the old, worn cutter in his left.

Ben reached over and tapped the back of Phillip's monitor. "I don't think you'll be needing this today."

"Oh, okay." Phillip nodded, closed his laptop, and slid it back into its case. "So where do we go from here, Mr. Ben?"

"Funny. I was about to ask you the same question," Ben said as he smiled and pointed the end of his cigar toward Phillip. "We've covered a lot of ground together. You have a bunch of questions to answer and a lot for your organization to execute. So what do you hope the outcome will be from all the time we've spent?"

"Increased sales revenue, my friend! Higher margins. Kicking our competitors' rear ends," Phillip said enthusiastically. "This company has been stalled for years, since way before I got involved. They had a lot of the raw materials needed for success when I took over but didn't have all the right pieces in the right places. Now we're providing the process and structure to help our people be the best in the industry. We're going to rule, my man!"

"I certainly hope so, son. We've both wanted something to come from this all along," Ben said as he looked down at the baseball resting on Phillip's napkin. "Unfortunately, what's ahead of you isn't an easy task. And it's why Newton's laws of motion popped into my head yesterday."

"I'm dying to know. What do Newton's laws have to do with sales transformation? Time to connect the dots again, Ben." Now it was Phillip's turn to sit back in his chair, watch, and listen.

"When I saw the ball, I thought of the game first," Ben said as he looked toward the fields. "The ball at rest meant the game was over. That's what started the mental chain reaction that leads us here.

"Everything you and I have talked about since Chairman Bill's fish fry was represented by that ball sitting in the grass way out in center field. It reminded me that what I know about running sales organizations has been sitting still, obscured by some pretty tall grass, until I met you." Ben picked up his cigar and held it to his lips. Phillip watched as three small puffs of smoke swirled upward. He hoped he would have the opportunity to see that happen many more times.

"So I helped you find the ball," Phillip said proudly.

"Not exactly. That's where Sir Isaac comes in. A body at rest will remain at rest unless an outside force acts on it," Ben said as he reached over and nudged the baseball. "You were the outside force that acted on the truths of sales transformation. You started them in motion."

Phillip smiled broadly. "When we first met in the board's waiting room, either the grass was too tall for me to see the ball, or I just wasn't looking hard enough."

Ben returned the smile. "You were focused on making the team, son. At that moment, you didn't care about the ball."

"True," Phillip said in agreement.

"So now the ball is sitting still on the table, just like everything you've learned is sitting still in a file on your laptop," Ben said as he pointed at Phillip's computer case. "The truth is, nothing will happen unless you cause it to be put in motion. The ball is in your hands now, son. It is up to you to keep it in motion. You have an incredible responsibility."

"I feel it, Ben. Northing will happen unless I keep this moving. None of this will have any impact whatsoever if I let it sit in the tall grass," Phillip said as he looked at the ball.

"It is never-ending, my dear friend, and I want you to keep this ball as a reminder. Every single thing we've talked about since our first meeting is an obstacle that can stop the forward motion of sales transformation. You have to be a greater force." Ben rested his cigar.

"It is a huge undertaking, Ben. I know it will take a lot of work."

"And that leads us to another of Newton's laws of motion. I think it's his second," Ben said as he held up two fingers. "Acceleration is produced when a force acts on a mass. The greater the mass, the greater the amount of force needed."

Ben picked up the baseball and tossed it a few inches in the air, catching it and tossing again and again. "This ball would be a better example of the force required to accelerate sales transformation if it were several times larger and made of lead. The effort not only has to be constant, it has to be strong."

"I am committed, Ben. I can't wait to see the impact on sales and margins. I'm obsessed," Phillip said.

"I hope that impact happens, son. If you focus on the right things, it surely will," Ben said as he placed the baseball back on the table. "Remember earlier I told you that the last thing I thought about was getting that ball back to where it could do what it was made to do?"

"I think that was the fourth or fifth thing your twisted little mind thought of when you spotted the ball," Phillip said with a grin.

"It's one a my greatest concerns, Phil, and precisely why this final lesson is so important. It's making certain the truths you've learned get back to a place where they can do what they were made to do," Ben said as he tapped the top of the baseball with two fingers.

"You see, some salespeople and sales managers spend their entire lives chasing deals, contracts, attainment of quota, commissions, money, sales," Ben said with more than a touch of sadness in his voice. "Revenue and margin targets control their lives. They believe it's the focus, the end point, the desired result. It becomes an obsession. The shame is a lot of them fail because they and their companies are obsessed with the wrong thing. To become a trusted partner to your customers, revenue and margins can't be the only thing, or even the primary thing, you're after."

Ben's statement was the point of a needle striking Phillip's balloon. The popping sound was almost audible. He looked directly at Ben and listened as intently as he ever had.

As Ben spoke, he noticed Phillip's fingers were continually rubbing the surface of the worn cigar cutter. That was exactly what Ben wanted.

"What a lot of them fail to realize is, in business, the amount of money you make is directly proportional to the amount of impact you have on other people. The greater the depth and breadth of the impact, the more money you make. Hitting revenue targets, increasing margins, and kicking competitors' butts are all by-products of impact, period, end of story. So what should we all be chasing? What should all salespeople and the companies they work for be obsessed with, Phil?"

"There is no question, Ben. Impacting lives." Phillip felt the rush of revelation he had gotten used to in his conversations with Ben.

"That, my dear friend, is huge. If you want to transform your organization from being just one more vendor on the preferred list, into a trusted partner and advisor, your entire organization has to focus on finding ways to have greater impact on others." Ben paused to allow Phillip time to reflect.

"And it's not just you and your salespeople impacting your customers, Phil. That may be what generates revenue, but the chain has links from your senior management all the way to the center of your customers' businesses. That has been a common theme in every lesson you've learned.

"Get this, son. The most obvious thing we've talked about is everyone in your organization focusing on impacting your customers' businesses in meaningful, measurable ways. The subtle, underlying message is that there has to be a focus on positively impacting people within your organization as well," Ben said with common sense finality.

"You are so right, Ben," Phillip said as lifted his cigar and took three quick, Ben-like puffs without inhaling. He watched the smoke rise as he had Ben's many times before. "We'll only realize the revenue and margin impact of transformation when we've found ways to have greater impact on each other and our customers."

"That's the truth, my friend. Senior managers have to be focused on impacting everyone in the organization. They have a greater probability of accomplishing that if they find ways to impact the lives of the people who report to them. In turn, the next level of management down should look for ways to positively impact the people they're responsible for. That continues all the way to field level management and salespeople. If you all do your jobs right and hold each other accountable, that will manifest itself in the entire organization being a better partner to each other and, ultimately, to your customers." Ben leaned forward, reached across the table and put his hand on Phillip's hand. "And that, Phillip Evan Hawthorne, is a big part of your final lesson."

As Phillip was listening to Ben, he didn't realize he had been turning the cutter in his hand, rubbing it with his fingers. It actually didn't occur to him until Ben touched the hand Phillip was holding it in. The cutter felt oddly familiar, comfortable, like he had held it before. He wondered if it looked so worn because others had handled it that way.

"I'm always amazed, Ben," Phillip said sincerely. He had long gotten used to shaking his head in wonderment as he spoke with Ben. "As we were competing for the CSO position, I remember thinking how ridiculous it was that the board was considering you to lead them through sales transformation. I mean, come on and admit it, Ben. Have you ever transformed a sales organization?"

"Never needed to. I had an incredible mentor who taught me, from very early on in my sales career, how to do the right things in the right way. None of the lessons I've passed on have been new, Phil. The only reason companies are trying to transform their sales organizations now is that they somehow got off track. They are simply trying to go back to universal truth, the things that have always been, and always will be, right."

"You said a moment ago that this idea of impact was a big part of my lesson tonight. I'm glad it's not the whole thing, Ben. I'm still holding this cigar cutter," Phillip said while holding his prized gift up, directly between him and Ben. "When I opened the box and took this out, you told me it would mean a whole lot more to me by the time we left. What did you mean?"

"I told you the cigar cutter hasn't always been mine, Phil. I've had it for around twenty-seven years. The guy who taught me how to use a cigar as a timer gave it to me." Ben held up his Montecristo. "I told you this was the cigar he used. He was my mentor. Most of what you've heard came from him. For over a quarter century and through every sales and management position I have held, that cigar cutter has been a reminder. Now it's yours."

"You've never talked about this mentor. Who taught you? Who was this dude? This guy was way ahead of his time."

"It was your dad, Phil."

Phillip was briefly paralyzed by the answer.

And for what seemed like eternity, Ben said nothing else. Phillip was overwhelmed by the silence so loud, so deafening. In an instant, he thought he might laugh, cry, run, scream, or tell Ben he was crazy. All he could do was sit and stare. He continued to look directly at Ben and listen, but later realized it was at that moment he learned what it meant to stare through somebody. It became his lifetime reference for an out-of-body experience.

As Phillip fought back tears, Ben continued. "I'm sure you're fully aware of this, son, but your father was an amazing man—profoundly logical, sensible, rational, wise, a brilliant salesperson and sales leader."

Just as what seemed like minutes or even hours when dreaming actually happened in seconds, so did the memories that began to flash through Phillip's mind as Ben talked—conversations with his dad, his stories, his lessons. He suddenly recalled most all of them ending as his dad was putting out a cigar. The timer! Phillip thought the end of his dad's lessons and the end of his cigars had been nothing more than coincidence. No wonder he had been so comfortable so quickly with Ben.

"Really, Ben. Say it again. Are you telling me all this was my father's? Everything we've talked about?" Phillip was still in shock, disbelief.

"No, Phillip. No one owns what your dad and I, and now you, know. It is simply universal truth, passed from person to person, generation to generation," Ben said as he gently placed his cigar on the corner of the table. "Your dad was a humble man. I will tell you that in all of my conversations with him, he never claimed ownership of any of this. He only claimed to be the messenger."

"How did this happen? How did you know him?" Phillip asked as he wiped a tear from the side of his face.

"Your father was my first sales manager, Phil. Man, what a blessing that turned out to be. I learned the right way from day one. I never picked up a lot of the bad habits you and I've talked about. Your dad made certain of that." The respect Ben had for Phillip's father came through clearly in his voice.

"How long did you know him? How old were you? How old was my dad?" Ben had caused Phillip's mind to race before, but now it was in over-drive.

"About thirteen years, Phil. But it always seemed like I had known him my whole life." Ben smiled as he reminisced. "Your dad was forty-two when you were born, right?"

"That's right."

"I met him just before you were born. I was a child. At least that's what I call twenty-five-year-olds nowadays. Your dad took me under his wing. Heck, he took everyone under his wing. I was as green as they come and he wanted to make certain I got it right from the start so I wouldn't have to 'transform' later in my career." Ben watched as Phillip unconsciously rubbed the old cigar cutter with his thumbs.

"I think your dad sensed something was about to happen before the accident," Ben said as he looked toward the Little League fields. "In the weeks before he passed, we would come here before your games to talk about selling. It's as if he wanted to make certain I carried these truths with me if anything ever happened to him."

Phillip stared at the fields with Ben. "He was only fifty-four when he died."

"I know, Phillip." Ben said while turning back to Phillip. "Your dad and I were here at this café the day before he passed. You were about to play a Little League game. It was at this very spot that we had the same conversation you and I are having now. It was about the obligation to carry all of this forward. Your father felt very strongly that no matter where I went or who I worked for, these principles had to go with me."

"I'm in shock," Phillip said as he looked down at the cigar cutter.

Ben leaned forward toward Phillip. "I lost track of you after your dad was laid to rest. I had no idea you had chosen selling as a career. Considering the gene pool that produced you, I could have figured. The day I found out we were competing for the same position, I knew that fate had caused our paths to cross. I still think your dad had a hand in putting us in that waiting room together. There was no question you were the right man for the job. You just needed a little of the knowledge and skills I'm sure your dad would have passed on to you if things had worked out differently. I owed it to him to make sure you got it."

Ben reached over to Phillip and, as a father would, patted Phillip on the knee and looked him squarely in the eyes. "It's your turn, son."

Phillip, once again, looked down at the cutter in his hands and began to feel a rush of emotion that was strong enough for Ben to sense. As he held it between his thumb and index finger and raised it slowly, Phillip began to smile.

"Yep, Phillip. Your dad gave me that cutter as a reminder of our conversations and my obligation to use what I had learned to impact the lives of others. Like everything we've talked about, it is meant to be passed on. I now sincerely believe he knew you would have it one day."

"It feels so comfortable in my hand, Ben," Phillip said while examining the cutter from all directions. "Now I know why. I remember sometimes holding it as my dad told stories. Wow. Why didn't you tell me this before?"

"I wanted you to hear the lessons as your dad would have taught them, Phil, without the emotion that may have clouded their meaning for you. It's the same way they were taught to me and exactly the way you should pass them on." Ben picked up his cigar and took a single draw.

"Your dad sought the truth about selling and running sales organizations. He gathered these truths from his customers, people he worked for, people who worked for him, from TV ads for exercise machines to African proverbs and Little League baseball fields. To him, it was all part of the universal truth of impacting other people's lives in meaningful, measurable ways."

"It's funny now how so much is coming back to me," Phillip said as he turned toward the baseball fields. "I really think my dad was trying to teach me some of these lessons indirectly when I was a kid. I'm sure that's one of the reasons I accepted so much of what you've taught me so quickly. Dad had greased the skids.

"Once in a while he would be at practice and hear the coach tell me what I needed to work on. The next Sunday, when Dad would be off and there were no games or practices, he and I would play baseball and work on whatever it was the coach wanted me to improve. He talked about how my behaviors impacted my performance and ultimately the success of the team. I always walked into Monday's practice and the coach would see me do something 100 percent better than a few days before. Dad was exposing gaps, determining the cause, and helping me correct my problems. He cared enough to listen to what the coach wanted me to work on and insisted I play baseball, like I should do everything else—the right way."

"Your dad didn't know any other way. Truth is truth and right is right." Between the two of them, Ben and Phillip had heard those words come from the mouth of Phillip Evan Hawthorne Sr. dozens, maybe hundreds of times before.

"I have no idea how long I will have this cigar cutter, but I know it won't be forever. I have a feeling my dad got it from a mentor that you and I will never know," Phillip said as he held the cutter tightly. "This is part of its journey. I've become the carrier, the messenger, just like you and Dad."

"You've just spoken the truth, son. Your dad would be so proud."

"I'm sure he is, Ben."

Ben held up his right index finger. "Before we go, I have one more question to add to your list. Your dad used to ask it in sales meetings, in operations reviews, even when he helped evaluate opportunities with his sales reps. It's the most important question of all. As a matter of fact, you can be certain sales transformation will have not taken place until you can answer yes to this question."

"I'm ready, Ben," Phillip said as he leaned forward in anticipation.

"Do your customers truly consider you and company a trusted partner and advisor?"

Phillip nodded slowly. "We can't say we have transformed until our customers tell us we have. They are the final judge."

"That, once again, my friend, is the absolute truth."

Ben extinguished his cigar and stood, holding out his arms. Phillip got up from his chair and hugged Ben as he would have hugged his father had he been given one more opportunity. At that moment, he realized the anxiety he felt coming to this meeting was connected to the feeling of abandonment he experienced with his father's passing. He didn't want to lose Ben.

As if he had been able to read Phillip's mind and emotions, Ben said, "We will keep in contact, son. I believe we have a lot to accomplish together, many lives to impact, so much to pass forward. There is no reason for it to stop here."

And without another word, Ben stepped back, patted Phillip on the shoulder, went to his car to grab a worn Little League baseball, and headed across the street to the fields where he would put it back in motion doing what it was intended to do.

Phillip remained at the café table marveling at this collection of lessons on sales transformation. A tartar sauce-making county commission chairman, a 1965 Ford Mustang, a British talent show judge, an African wise man, a homebuilder, two Little League baseball coaches, Sir Isaac Newton, a crafty old messenger named Ben Delaney and Phillip's own father were contributors. How remarkable.

He opened his laptop and clicked on a file labeled "AXIOMS of Sales Transformation." In front of him was the roadmap, a simple list of questions that needed to be answered with a "yes" if sales transformation was going to take place. Phillip read each one slowly.

1. Have you clearly defined a formal process by which everyone in your organization sells?

2. Has every part of your process passed the test of being a universally accepted truth?

3. Is the process focused on expanding the value you deliver the customers through the sales engagement?

4. Have you piloted the process with a broad spectrum of your sales team, not just the underperformers, to make certain it is applicable and accepted by all?

5. Do all of your salespeople believe the formal sales process will produce significant impact on their own sales, margins, and income?

6. Is your sales process dynamic enough to allow for the uniqueness of your customers and changes in your competitive landscape?

7. Can your formal sales process stand the test of time by supporting changes in your product and service portfolio?

8. Does your formal sales process provide a foundation for your salespeople to understand the customer's business first?

9. Are your salespeople talking to a broad spectrum of people in your customer's business outside of IT and/or purchasing?

10. Can your salespeople tell you the vision, goals, plans, processes, strengths, weaknesses, etc., of their customers outside the realm of your company's products and services?

11. Are you or your salespeople regularly invited to your customer's business to discuss their driving business issues as a strategic partner *before* there is an obvious need for what you sell?

12. Have you tested your trainers to make certain they have the skills necessary to train salespeople?

13. Does your instructor training include them proving they can demonstrate new skills in a compelling and believable fashion to their internal customer, your salespeople?

14. Are your formal sales process and training delivery designed to facilitate incremental improvement over time? In other words are they developed to improve one skill at a time over time?

15. Is your formal sales process completely integrated with your systems such as sales force automation, customer relationship management, and any other sales and management programs?

16. Do your systems and management tools include measurement of behavioral change and not just results?

17. Are your marketing programs and materials completely aligned to and in support of your sales process?

18. Have all managers, including senior leaders, attended training and fully committed to your formal sales process and management methodology?

19. Have you and your managers clearly defined activity and proficiency metrics for every individual on your sales team?

20. Do your managers consistently review those metrics to uncover gaps in performance?

21. Do your managers, from field level to C-level, hold themselves and everyone on their team accountable for the required changes in behavior?

22. Can senior managers effectively examine and evaluate the behaviors of people in your organization to ensure the required behavioral changes are actually taking place?

23. Do your senior managers actively seek and report successes with sales transformation?

24. Are your senior managers creating programs that encourage everyone in the organization to find ways to be the best partner for your customers?

Phillip placed his hands on the laptop keyboard and, in all caps, typed:

25. DO YOUR CUSTOMERS TRULY CONSIDER YOU AND YOUR COMPANY A TRUSTED PARTNER AND ADVISOR?

Phillip smiled as he saved the file and closed his laptop. He extinguished his cigar, the first of many more to come, and continued his journey to sales transformation. He couldn't wait to take others with him.

Epilogue

Phillip Evan Hawthorne worked hard to make certain he and his company could answer yes to all twenty-five questions about sales transformation. His company became the global leader in their business segment while being considered by their customers as trusted partners and advisors. Phillip became recognized as a leading authority on sales transformation and ended up recording the wisdom that Ben, Phil's father, and others had collected by writing a book entitled *The Truth about Sales Transformation, 25 AXIOMS for Becoming a Trusted Partner to Your Customers.*

Ben Delaney helped Chairman Bill build a tartar sauce empire. From the proceeds of his success with condiments, he opened "Stogies and Stories," a small cigar shop next to his favorite café where you can find Ben most afternoons surrounded by business people, including newly employed CSO David Malone, listening intently to stories about things like tartar sauce, African proverbs, talent show judges, and Sir Isaac Newton. In his spare time, he coaches Little League.

Author Bio

Bob Nicols Jr. has 34 years of experience in sales, sales management, executive management and sales force development. He founded Burton Training Group, now AXIOM Sales Force Development, in 1990 after being a top and highly recognized performer in sales, sales management and executive positions within the technology sector. He has managed and mentored thousands of sales people, sales managers and senior managers and been responsible for hundreds of millions of dollars in sales. For more than 21 years he has developed and delivered sales programs that have become the standard for many Fortune 100 companies. AXIOM programs have been implemented in over 30 countries including Japan, the UK, Germany, Dubai, Brazil, India, Taiwan, Singapore, Australia, China, Mexico, Canada, South Korea, Slovakia, Sweden, and The Netherlands. He is a trusted advisor to the presidents and senior managers of multiple organizations, both large and small and has been a board member of a national technology company. Bob's highly energetic and insightful lectures and workshops have resulted in invitations to be a featured presenter at dozens of national and international sales meetings and conferences.

Made in the USA
Charleston, SC
26 September 2013